Human Sexuality:
A Christian View

John C. Dwyer

Sheed & Ward

Sheed & Ward™ is a service of National Catholic Reporter Publishing,
Inc.

Library of Congress Catalog Number: 87-61923

ISBN: 1-55612-076-1

Published by: Sheed & Ward
           115 E. Armour Blvd. P.O. Box 414292
           Kansas City, MO 64141-4292

To order, call: (800) 821-7926

Contents

Foreword

Sexuality is both fascinating and troubling. It is fascinating because it is at once a universal dimension of the human experience and at the same time a uniquely mysterious domain—a domain where we experience existence with an intensity which can only awaken awe and wonder. Our sexuality is troubling because it is an area of life in which, more often than we care to admit, we experience sin and guilt (or, if we have tried to banish both from our lives, an area in which we experience a vague and indefinable malaise). The biblical narrative of the temptation and fall of our first parents has often been interpreted as though the forbidden fruit were sexual pleasure, and this may be closer to the origins of this mythical account than many are aware of: the snake was a sexual symbol in the myths and rituals of the peoples among whom the stories recorded in Genesis arose.

Sex is therefore in every sense a *mysterium tremendum et fascinosum*—a mystery which awakens feelings of awe, and even fear and anxiety; and yet it is the mystery which is intriguing and all-absorbing. It seems to promise that transcendence of ourselves which is our deepest human desire and yet it makes us painfully aware of our limits and of the supreme difficulty of finding ourselves in the process of losing ourselves.

The very terms in which we speak of sex here already foreshadow the uneasy relationship of religion and sexuality. At times, religion has used sexuality; sexual activities have been surrounded with religious ritual, and in many religions the orgiastic element is prominent. But at least as often, religion has feared sex and stamped it as demonic, treating it as the domain of darkness and evil from which religion is called to save us. Sex treads on ground which religion calls its own and which it is unwilling to share, particularly with a sector of life as omnipresent and as fascinating as sex.

The relationship of Christianity to sexuality has been particularly troubled. For the other great monotheistic religions, Judaism and Islam, sexuality is a natural good, and, by and large, Jews and Moslems have a relatively relaxed and healthy relationship with this aspect of life. But because of its teaching on the incarnation, Christianity cannot see sexuality as a merely natural good. Because God revealed himself definitively in one human being, all that is authentically human is a revelation of God. On the one hand, Christianity cannot divinize nature; the gods have been driven from earth and sky, from forest glades and from the storms that scour the earth, and from the still more powerful forces which drive men and women to seek in each other the fulfillment of their dreams. But on the other hand, if the gods have been driven from nature, still, all of nature reveals the one God, who not only transcends the world but who dwells within it. Christian faith is called to maintain this puzzling paradox, and to bear the burden of this trying tension.

But this difficult relationship between Christianity and sexuality has been compounded by events which have nothing to do with the origins or the essence of Christian faith but have much to do with the way in which that faith developed when it left the land of its birth and turned to the gentile world. In the course of history, these events have given Christianity a pronounced anti-sexual bias.

However, this book is not a history of the troubled relationship of religion and sexuality. Rather, it is an attempt to reflect on the phenomenon of sexuality from the standpoint of what is really central and essential to Christianity—that is, the view of God and of the human condition which became real in the words and in the life of Jesus of Nazareth. The book tries to answer this question: if we take Christianity seriously, how do we think about our sexuality and what do we do about it?

This book draws on the ethical reflections of many thinkers, Christian and non-christian. It draws on much modern work in psychology and motivation theory. Finally, it is the expression of what I think theology is (or should be): the attempt to talk intelligently about God and about the relationship of God to every area of human existence and especially to those aspects of life which are near the center of the human personality.

For much in this book, I am indebted to my students, and, among them, especially to Greg Stakich and Vanessa Carrow. My dear friends, John and Marg Hills, read early drafts of the work and have accompanied it with their constant encouragement as it approached its present form. For many reasons, some self-evident and some known only to me, the book would never have been written, were it not for my wife, Odile. Finally, I am dedicating the book to an outstanding moral theologian from whom I have learned much, and whose wisdom, humor, and deep human sympathy have made him an extraordinary teacher and a cherished friend: Rev. James O'Donohoe, of Boston College.

Platte Clove, NY
John Charles Dwyer

1.

Introduction: Some Basic Concepts and a Bit of History

A Theological View of Human Sexuality

It may seem strange to propose a *theological* view of human sexuality, but it is an approach which makes good sense, if we are clear about what theology is. Theology is not airy speculation, suitable for those with a taste for abstraction. It is rather *the act of putting intelligence at the service of faith*. Many people are puzzled by this definition, because they cannot imagine how it is possible for intelligence and faith to be related in any way. Some feel this way because they despise what they call "faith" and find in it nothing more than wishful thinking and a flight from reason and responsibility: stances which are unworthy of an intelligent human being. Others feel that faith and intelligence cannot be related because they despise intelligence, and see in it nothing more than an arrogant attempt to live in a world without God. Neither of these groups will find this book to their liking, because it is written in the conviction that faith and intelligence, far from being in competition for our loyalty, are really dependent on each other. Faith needs intelligence in order to become what it is called to be and in order to extend its influence over the whole life of the believer. But at the same time, the commitment to intelligence, the firm will to understand, is already a kind of rudimentary but real act of faith. Genuine faith does not compete with intelligence; genuine faith makes it possible for us to understand God and therefore to understand the world, other persons, and ourselves.

To propose a theological view of human sexuality is really to make several tacit assertions, of which two are most important. First, it asserts that sexuality is a facet or dimension of our lives which should be *understood*. This does not mean that it should be reduced to a set of logical conclusions, but it does mean that we should be aware of ourselves as sexual, sexed beings, aware of this facet of our lives in all of its reality and all of its mystery. Second, to propose a theological view of sexuality is to affirm that, since we are really human to the extent to which we stand consciously in the presence of God, only a theological view of sexuality can do justice to this extremely important part of our lives.

Obviously, many people are not willing to admit that God has anything to do with human life (and many are unwilling even to admit that "God is there"), but this book might be of interest to them for another reason. If they find that the approach to human sexuality which is outlined here makes good sense, then they might conclude either that there is something wrong with the methods of thinking and reasoning employed, or that their own rejection of God (or of God's connection with human life) should be reexamined. To put it another way: an intelligent view of human sexuality might turn out to be an interesting way of raising the question of God.

This book is not interested solely in an ethical or moral view of sexuality, although, if these terms are rightly understood, it will include both. However, our concern is more general and more universal; we are simply interested in the meaning of the fact that we exist as men or as women. Obviously, there are many levels of meaning in human sexuality, but a theological view of sexuality is concerned about its ultimate meaning, and is interested in all of the other meanings of human sexuality in so far as they are rooted or grounded in this one. In fact, it is the concern for ultimate meaning which makes the view of sexuality presented here theological, for the question of God is not really the question of whether or not there is a supreme being; the question of God is the question of whether or not human life has ultimate meaning. Anyone who holds that it does is already at least a "secret" believer in God. Furthermore, as we will see in the following pages, to assert that human sexuality has ultimate meaning is to affirm that it touches our existence precisely in so far as we are persons, and that because each of us exists as man or as woman, the love which defines us as persons, and the love through which we foster life and growth in others, is a distinctively manly or womanly love.

While dealing with basic matters here, one very important point must be made. This book is written in the conviction that in all areas of human life there are some ways or patterns of acting which are helpful in attaining the ends and goals of human life, and there are other ways or patterns of acting which violate the meaning of human life. Human life *has* a meaning, and it has goals and purposes which are *there,* whether we know it and like it or not. We *ought* to choose actions which promote the attainment of these goals and we *ought* to avoid actions which hinder their attainment. In other words, the view of human existence (and therefore of our sexuality) which is presented in this book is deliberately judgmental: that is, it intends, among other things, to make possible correct judgments about our own conduct and the conduct of others—judgments which are not afraid to use the words "right" and "wrong," "good" and "bad." The refusal, in principle, to make such judgments, that is, the denial that we and others can do wrong, is not motivated by genuine esteem for freedom, but rather by a deep contempt for the human being, which expresses itself in trivializing the human condition by denying that we have the power to do great good and great evil. Our human grandeur is closely connected with the fact that we can rise to great heights and fall to great depths. We have enormous possibilities for good and for evil, and we create ourselves in the choices we make.

Sexuality as a Gift of God

It is very easy to misunderstand the relationship of God to human sexuality and particularly the relationship of God to questions of right and wrong in sexual conduct. In many religious traditions, sex is governed by strict laws and taboos. It is seen as the domain in life where sin is lurking and where the sins committed are particularly evil. This approach has done so much harm that it would probably be a good thing to avoid using the word "law" in speaking of the relationship between God and human sexuality (even though, when carefully defined, the word can be used accurately and correctly). The basic theological statement about human sexuality is not that God has legislated about it, but rather that God wants us to exist this way. We exist as men or as women, our personal existence is sexual, and this is in accord with the will of God. The differentiation of the sexes, and all of the results of this differentiation, have come about because God wanted it and intended it.

We might note that this is evident simply from the fact that human life evolved from prehuman forms which were successful because of their development of sexual reproduction during long eons of evolution, but those willing to make use of the Bible as a source have a much more interesting argument at their disposal in the text of *Genesis* 1:27: "God made the human being in his image and likeness; in the image of God he made them; male and female he made them." This text not only asserts that sexual differentiation (the fact that each of us is called to the "other," to the "thou" of the opposite sex) is the result of God's creative will. Even more, it asserts that the meaning of humanity is not contained in man alone or in woman alone, but in man *and* woman, precisely in so far as they are in dialogue with each other. And finally, it asserts that it is precisely in the dialogue of man and woman with each other, in their mutual relationship with and their dependence on each other, that they are made in the image and likeness of God. And therefore, their dialogue, on all levels, is one very important way in which God is revealed.[1]

Two very important conclusions can be drawn from the fact that our sexuality is God's gift to us. First, sex is not to be confused with God, and the exercise of our sexual powers is not of *absolute* value. Pansexualism, or the divinization of sex, is not genuinely human, and it does not reflect a real understanding of the place of sexuality in our lives. This divinizing of sex, this treating of sex as the ultimate value in life has been a common enough phenomenon in many periods of history and it is quite prevalent today. One of its symptoms is the nervous preoccupation with maximizing sexual pleasure and a virtual obsession with the orgasm. Many of the sexual taboos which appear in different cultures and many of the sexual rituals which appear in connection with religion have their origin in this divinization of sex. Some of these religions surround sex with ritual because they see it as the place where the divine powers are accessible to us (and where they threaten us as well). To call our sexuality the gift of God is to say something extremely positive about it, but it is also to deny both divinity and ultimacy to sexual activity in itself.

But there is a second very important consequence of the fact that our sexuality is a gift of God: sex is not demonic. Our sexuality is not the place in our lives where evil forces are manifest; sex is not dirty, shameful, or impure. As we will see in the course of the book, this "demonizing" of sex is much more common today than we might suspect, and it is by no means restricted to those with puritanical leanings. Paradoxically, the tendency to demonize sex is not very different from the tendency to divinize it. To use mythical terminology, in one case sex is the place where we meet the gods above, the gods of light; in the other case, sex is the place where we meet the gods below, the gods of darkness. Incidentally, the peculiar tendency, of which there are traces in almost every culture, to stamp sex as "dirty" in some ambiguous sense, almost certainly originates in the fact that our neuroses and psychoses find a fertile field of activity here. But, as we will note later, this is the case, not because there is something "wrong" with sexuality as such, but rather because our sexuality is so central to our personal existence.

However, there is another attitude which is sometimes mistaken for shame or embarrassment in regard to our sexuality, but which has very different roots and which is the expression of a very positive value: that is, an attitude of reticence and reserve in speaking about our sexuality, because it is the place where the center of our personality is engaged and revealed in a peculiarly intense way. Vitality and creativity are manifest here in a mysterious and intriguing way, and this mystery should be respected and preserved, even while being revealed. Our sexuality is a domain of charm, beauty, depth, and power, and it should not be trivialized. The automation or mechanization of our sexuality is bad for us, and so is the incessant babbling about sex which is so common today.

The most important conclusion to be drawn from the fact that our sexuality is the gift of God, is simple but far-reaching: we ought to accept our sexuality and rejoice in it as the gift of God which it is. We ought to do this without anxiety but with great inner peace, because in accepting this gift we honor the one who gives it. As in the case of all such "simple" conclusions, much of a lifetime could be spent in implementing it and in living our lives in accord with it, but such conclusions are no less worthwhile because of this. A truth which is simple but profound is always very productive in life, if we pause to ponder it.

Understanding Our Sexuality

Our task as human beings is to act rightly and well. We fulfill this task, not precisely by obeying laws or regulations, but by being attentive to the real world in which we live, and by striving to understand and therefore respect the persons and things which make up this world. Above all, we do this by striving to understand the purposiveness of life and the goals which are inherent in persons, institutions, and things, so that we may act responsibly toward them. If we want to act rightly and well as sexual beings, we will do so by coming to understand the immanent purposes and goals which are essential to human sexuality. This demands careful and critical thought.

This does not suggest that our task is to "intellectualize" our sexuality, as though by making it more "intellectual" we would succeed in making it less sexual (which some apparently perceive as desirable). There is no question here of turning the cold light of disembodied intellect on our sexuality. Because we are human, our intelligence properly operates in close conjunction with our emotional life. This does not mean that it is a good thing to act irrationally, or to pay no attention to evidence or to facts. The emotional sector of life, properly understood, is not the domain of irrational feeling; genuine emotion is the experience of the beauty and charm of some part of the real world which is revealing itself to us. Emotion is the experience of the harmony (or its absence) of something which we understand, and it is emotion itself which impels us to deepen that act of understanding; emotion and intelligence belong together. Emotion is our response as persons to that which we have begun to understand, and we exercise our intelligence by being intrigued with the real world and by loving it in all of its complexity and its splendor. Genuinely human intelligence is profoundly emotional; genuine human emotions are profoundly intelligent. Without the exercise of this kind of intelligence, we cannot exist authentically. We are truly human only when we are present to ourselves with an awareness which is at once intelligent and emotional.

Of course, this call for careful and critical thought about our sexuality should not be confused with the deadly serious attitude we occasionally encounter in those who write about sex. They sometimes give the impression that at the moment of orgasm, one should be pondering the ultimate meaning of total commitment. Such nonsense is not a frequent temptation, but it is important to note that such an attitude ignores the spontaneity which is an essential part of the human sexual experience, and therefore it can contribute nothing to the attempt to understand the meaning of human sexuality.

The Christian Tradition

The role of Christian tradition in helping us to understand our sexuality is, at best, ambiguous. The general reflections on human conduct which were developed by the scholastic thinkers of the thirteenth century and by the leading moral theologians from the sixteenth century to the present, are not only valuable; they are indispensable. Within this tradition, theologians developed ways of asking questions and ways of finding answers which are essential for an understanding of our sexuality. However, when these theologians turned directly to the question of human sexuality, they often drew conclusions which have come increasingly under fire during recent years, and not without reason. In fact, in all of the Christian churches, warped attitudes about sexuality were quite prevalent; and this made it difficult to think and talk intelligently about sex.

The problem was serious in Catholic theology, because of the preoccupation of moral theologians with sin and because of their view of sex as an area where one might commit sin, and usually did. There was one principal reason for this: the textbooks in moral theology were written primarily for the training of future priests in the hearing of confessions, and in accord with the theology of the time, these books laid great emphasis on the ability to identify sins, to classify them by type, and to determine their relative gravity. However, regardless of this fact, to see sexuality almost exclusively as an area where sin can be committed is an appalling distortion, and it must be admitted that in this respect, as in many others, the tradition of the Christian churches had to some extent an antisexual bias.

There are other reasons for this anti-sexual bias, and they have nothing to do with the Christian message itself. In the Greco-Roman world at the time at which Christianity began to spread throughout the Empire, sexual perversion was widespread, and this provoked a revulsion which could easily extend to sexuality itself. However, an even more important factor was the Platonism of the Greek and Latin Fathers (that is, leading theologians during the first five centuries). Platonism argued that the *really* real was the spiritual, the ideal, and that involvement with matter, the flesh, and the body represented a falling away from the purity of existence, into the dark domain of contamination and evil. As a consequence, the attitude of churchmen toward conjugal life has often been very negative. We should be aware of this attitude, because it has influenced all of us, at least indirectly. An attitude which is unhealthy and distorted cannot be Christian, and unless such attitudes are explicitly rejected, they will make a Christian view of sexuality difficult, if not impossible.

If we keep this in mind, it will be instructive to note some examples of the teaching of some of the Fathers and Doctors of the early church. In general they run the gamut from mild suspicion and distaste to violent hostility and revulsion. The best one can say for them is that they regard the physical side of sexuality as somewhat degrading and animallike, if not actually dirty.

Gregory of Nyssa, John Chrysostom, and Jerome were of the opinion that God had really wanted human beings to reproduce as the angels did, but, foreseeing the sin of Adam and Eve, had providentially equipped them with the reproductive organs of the animals which they would become through their sin. Ambrose (Augustine's mentor) regarded sexual intercourse (even between husband and wife!) as defiling, and asserted that for this reason, priests should never marry, because "the ministerial office must be kept pure and unspotted and it must never be defiled by sexual intercourse." Jerome told husbands, "If we abstain from sexual intercourse, we honor our wives; if we do not abstain, we insult them." Augustine could think of no better reason for performing the marital act in private than the fact that it was "shameful."[2] Augustine's views on this matter have been out of style in the church for a century or two, and this is a good thing. If they were not, churchmen would still be teaching that sexual intercourse during pregnancy was at least a venial sin, and that intercouse after menopause is also sinful. This is what Augustine taught, and he was followed by almost all of the authors who wrote booklets for the guidance of confessors through the medieval period, and by most of the great scholastic theologians of the middle ages.[3] How deep Augustine's antipathy to sex was, is evident from his view that, although a procreative purpose kept sexual intercourse from being seriously sinful, it still stained the soul, and hence it would be better if married people never exercised this right, even though this would mean the end of the human race. Pope Gregory the Great, writing about two hundred years after Augustine, said that the pleasure experienced in sexual intercourse was, in itself, seriously sinful, and that it only became less serious if done in marriage, and then only in order to procreate a child.[4]

In general, the Fathers of the church in both East and West who are cited here were conditioned by their dualistic Greek philosophy to see the body as the source of evil, and therefore to see the joy experienced in the body as sinful. They are strongly in favor of continence and virginity, because these are the states in which we most surely triumph over our sexual drives. Platonic and Stoic thought were shadowed by a profound sexual pessimism, and under their influence the Fathers of the church in both the east and the west had failed to note Paul's observation that marriage is a gift of divine grace.[5]

When we turn to the scholastic period, we find that Thomas Aquinas, the leading theologian of the thirteenth century, had similar views about sex. (Although, he was far more liberal than some of his predecessors, and declared that it was only a venial sin for married people to "use" (!) each other on the special feast days of the church.) He also held that sexual intercourse was at least venially sinful if performed for any other than two reasons: either for procreating a child, or because one's marriage partner has requested it; however, the request itself was sinful, if made for any other reason than to procreate a child. So that there could be no doubt about its basically animalistic nature, Thomas said of the sex act: "Animals lack reason. Hence in the sex act, man becomes like the animals, because the pleasure of the sex act and the fervor of concupiscence cannot be moderated by reason."[6] He also notes that "Since the man who is too ardent a lover of his wife acts against the good of marriage, he may in a sense be called an adulterer."[7] To put it simply, Thomas does not seem to recognize that sexual union might, in the proper circumstances, be *good* for human beings, and he seems unaware of the personal values inherent in human sexuality.[8] Thomas, of course, was not alone. In his own day his views were regarded as very liberal. Four hundred years after his time, in 1679, Pope Innocent XI decreed that anyone who said that it was not sinful to have intercourse for pleasure was a heretic.[9]

Until very recently these attitudes have been surprisingly widespread in the church. For example, Marc Oraison, a French priest and psychiatrist who has done excellent work in the field of moral theology, suggests to young married couples a "certain asceticism in regard to their sexuality," noting that from the very outset of their marriage they will have reasons for not falling prey to "the violence of instinct."[10] In another example, Cardinal Leon Suenens, former primate of Belgium (and an intelligent and open-minded churchman, with an impressive record at Vatican II and after) wrote: "The fact remains that the sexual instinct is rooted in the lower part of man's nature and remains influenced by it." He continues, "In itself, the sexual instinct is self-centered, looks out for its own interests, and rather tends to subjugate people to its own ends, without respect for their dignity and independence as persons. It makes people into mere means, to the point of enslaving them and making them captives."[11] Earlier in the same book he had asserted: "The sex instinct becomes more and more ruthless the more it is yielded to."[12] Finally, he gives some advice to married couples: "If young married couples limit their love-making, they will inevitably develop a better control of themselves because of this progressive training."[13]

Pius XII, who was pope from 1939 to 1958, made similar comments about sexuality in various encyclicals. Typically, in his address to the midwives in 1958, he condemned those who "avoid habitually the fecundity of their union, while at the same time continuing to satisfy their sensuality." A similar thought appears in the work of the German laywoman and religious thinker, Ida Görres. In her short book, *Laiengedanken zum Zölibat* (*Thoughts of a Lay Person on Celibacy*) she wrote, "In the domain of the sexual, at that point in nature which is most profoundly numinous, something is not quite right; here, nature is characterized by original sin in a special way."[14] This summarized a point which she had made a few pages earlier: "A certain revulsion toward the sexual realm comes from our repeated experience that it is the source of human suffering, of unhappiness, shame, fear, degradation, lying, self-deception, etc. This is the origin of the postulate that one who wants an untroubled life, a life which is integrated and enjoys true inner freedom, should avoid, or even flee from the whole domain of the sexual."[15]

There is a single theme which runs through even these relatively recent comments on human sexuality. It is the notion that, even in marriage, sex is basically self-indulgent, too physical, and needs some motive beyond the joy of intimacy to justify it. The assumption seems to be that only when sex is "spiritualized" (by which these writers seem to mean that it must be stripped of its physical expression!) can it be called "love." The notion that sexual intercourse between married people might be good in itself never seems to enter their heads.

It is certainly time for a change. In the past, unchristian philosophies have led Christians to despise the body and to despise the sexuality which is so integral a part of the body. In turn, this has led to an exaggerated exaltation of celibacy and virginity, and this has been a major factor in preventing the development of a truly Christian understanding of sexuality.

The Opposite Aberration

These views of sexuality were certainly distorted, but behind them lies a valid insight which is often ignored today: we can and do commit sin and we can be and are responsible for great harm in the sexual domain of life. The denial of the possibility of sin here springs from the refusal to see sexuality as an integral part of life, and even more from contempt for our sexuality, as we will see later. However, it is important to see that serious evil is possible in the domain of sexuality, not because there is something wrong, or wicked, or evil about sex, but rather because sexuality is so central to human life that the whole person, the whole self, is engaged and revealed here. The problem is not with sex as such, but with the whole person. Furthermore, although many of the views which Christians have held from the time of the Fathers to modern times, can only be called unhealthy, it would be absurd to suggest that because of this, we should now treat sex simply as "fun" (in the sense of entertainment, pleasurable distraction), which really has no connection with the kind of human beings we are. Frequently enough today the opinion is voiced that our sexual behavior has nothing to do with the kind of persons we "really" are. But as a matter of fact, it has very much to do with the kinds of persons we are, for the simple reason that our whole existence is sexual, and we cannot divorce sexual expression from the core of our lives as persons.

This "fun" view of sex is frequently advanced in the name of sexual liberation, and we are often urged (usually by those with pronounced and obvious psychological problems) to "get rid of our hangups." But this approach to sexuality has nothing to do with freedom; in fact, it is a parody of real freedom. The sexual revolution has had far more destructive effects on the revolutionaries themselves than on the sometimes antiquated views of sex against which they campaigned. There is considerable evidence that what has been touted as sexual freedom has resulted in serious personality disorientation among those who believed this nonsense. We should not be surprised at this, because if sex is regarded merely as a pleasurable distraction, it cannot be integrated into the personality. But when something as deeply personal as sex is denied this integration, then the personality suffers serious harm, and real freedom becomes an impossibility. Our sexuality is simply too near the center of our personal existence to allow it to be objectivized as "fun." To trivialize sex is to trivialize life, and this is destructive.

A Comprehensive View of Sexuality

Now that we have mentioned a few of the obstacles which stand in the way of an intelligent view of human sexuality, it will be well to state in general terms what the rest of this book proposes to do: it proposes to offer a view of sexuality which is *Christian, human, idealistic*, and *realistic*. (And I would suggest that each of these predicates, if taken seriously, implies the other three.)

The view here will be *Christian*, not because it will be based on sexual norms or directives which are enunciated in the New Testament. There is very little material in the New Testament which deals directly with the problems we will be discussing. The Christian message, as found in the New Testament, does not legislate about sex. What it does is to create new possibilities of existence, which can manifest themselves in our sexual lives, as well as in other areas of life. The Gospel offers authentic sexual existence because it offers freedom, and it offers freedom because it offers unconditional acceptance. The freedom which the Gospel offers is freedom from the fear, anxiety, pride, and pretense which prevent us from viewing the challenges of our sexuality intelligently, and therefore prevent us from facing these challenges responsibly. It should be just as obvious that to promote a Christian view of sexuality is not to suggest that Christians have always thought intelligently about sexuality; they often have not. But the failure of Christians in this area has not been caused by their dedication to the Gospel, but rather by the strong influence of unchristian philosophies. Obviously, to promote a Christian view of sexuality is not to suggest that nonChristians cannot think and act responsibly in this area of life; they can, and for the reason just given, they often act more responsibly than Christians. To put it simply, to argue for a Christian view of sexuality is to assert, unequivocally, that the Gospel offers a definitive kind of liberation to the human being, which is the only certain guide to clear thought and responsible action in this extremely important area of life.

The view of sexuality presented here will be *human*, because in all that we say and do, our human reality, in all of its dimensions, deserves respect. We are human beings, not angels, and therefore we belong to the animal world. We should be intrigued and fascinated by this fact. We should relish this kinship we have with the physical world, with the other animals, and with all of nature. We should cherish our bodies, because it is through them that we are receptive to all of the wonders of the world, and through them that we are spokes(wo)men for this world. It is a marvelous thing to have a body, and we should be immensely happy that we do.

The view of sexuality presented here will be *idealistic,* because our sexuality is given to us not simply as a fact but, more importantly, as a task and a challenge. As human beings, we are called on to create our *selves*. We have the power to respond to this call because, at the center of our being, we are gifted with a hunger and a longing to be genuine persons, and with an inkling as to what that involves. To act in a morally good way is to choose to think clearly about what it means to be this kind of person. To act in a morally bad way is to choose to remain in the dark about what this means. It is a good thing to be idealistic about our sexuality because there are enormous possibilities for personal growth, and therefore for commitment to the neighbor, in the sexual dimension of our lives. To say that human sexuality confronts us with a challenge is to assert that the personal integration of our sexuality is a very high ideal.

Finally, the view of sexuality presented here will be *realistic*. Irrational fear of sex has done much harm in the past, and this fear has often led to prudish and unrealistic ways of thinking and speaking of our sexuality. Our task of creating genuine selves and of achieving a truly personal integration of our sexuality has to start with the given, with the way we really are. In the domain of the sexual, as in all other areas of human life, the given is frequently confused, unhealthy, self-centered, and sinful. This is a situation which we have to face, and we should speak about it honestly. There is much in life that is ugly, but the first step in changing it is to examine it honestly.

The Contemporary Challenge

There is a pressing need today to think attentively, clearly, and critically about human sexuality. The old sexual ethic has collapsed (at least in the sense that it is not generally respected), and in some respects this is not a bad thing; but the pseudo-freedom which replaced it has often led to considerable confusion about the nature of manhood and womanhood, and it may be responsible for many of the sexual dysfunctions which seem so prevalent today, if the number of sex therapists and the sheer volume of talk-show babble are any indication.

There are serious obstacles to clear and critical thought in the area of sex, but the deliberate attempt to locate these obstacles and remove them can work wonders, and the healing power of such deliberately clear thinking is very great. Such thought does not remain in the theoretical realm but touches all of the problems which we face as sexual beings, as well as the broader question of the polar relationship of man and woman in all sectors of life. Only on the basis of the truth about who we are can we make statements about the human condition which are prescriptive and not merely descriptive. Perhaps surprisingly, we not only need such statements; we want them.

2.

Sexuality and the Person

The First Basic Fact about Human Sexuality

Clear and critical thought about human sexuality has to begin with one very important fact: human sexuality is *total* in every sense of the word. Human sexuality is total because it affects the whole human being. It is not simply a biological fact; it is psychological, emotional, and spiritual as well. Our sexuality is not something which we simply *have* or *possess*. Sometimes, at least, we can distance ourselves from our possessions, but we cannot distance ourselves from our sexuality; it is part of our *existence,* and for each of us it involves the "I," the center of the personality. There are many things, many situations in life which we can confront: poverty and wealth, health and sickness, the presence or absence of educational or economic opportunities. Many of these are very important, but in the strict sense they are outside of us. They certainly affect us, and we, in turn, may use them, react to them, and take stances toward them. When we do, these stances and attitudes are very important in determining the kind of persons that we are; but, in themselves, these different situations do not reach the most profound level of our

17

existence; we face them and we deal with them, but they are "outside" us and they cannot be identified with us.

Sexuality is different. For each of us, it is the "I" which exists as man or woman. As each of us utters the word "I," it is not a neuter or sexless spirit which speaks, not an essentially angelic being which happens to be immersed in a body whose sexuality is a purely animal phenomenon. Rather, when each of us speaks, it is the "I" itself which is sexual. We *are,* we *exist* as men or women, and this distinction goes to the very heart of our personal mystery. Sexuality is not a situation or condition to be confronted or used by the person; rather, it is in itself a form of personal existence. When our sexual existence is what it should be, it is a *personal* value, and it merits the respect and esteem which is owed to all authentic personal values.

Sexuality Is Inseparable from Personal Existence

This means that sexuality is not a distinct sector of life which can be isolated from the rest of our existence. The theological basis of this statement is the fact that God has created us as men and women, and that in our dialogue as men and women, on all levels, we reveal God. God is the one who, from all eternity, chose not to be alone; s/he is the one who loved us with an everlasting love before the world began; s/he is the one who has chosen to exist for us, to include us in the finality and the purposiveness of his own existence, and it is the love of God and that alone which keeps us in existence, moment by moment. Creation reveals this kind of God, and that is why the text of Genesis 1: 27, which we mentioned above, speaks of the creation of man *and* woman. It is precisely in the dialogue of man and woman that we symbolize and realize (in both senses: understand and make real) the truth that authentic existence is always existence for another. Our sexuality is the means chosen by God to reveal the truth that it is not good for the human being to be alone. The existence of the two sexes is a fundamental structure of human life; it is not simply a biological fact, but is rather the most basic way in which human beings are related to each other.[16]

We can never really separate ourselves from our sexuality, but even the attempt to do so is destructive in the extreme, for it is the attempt to take a part of our very selves and to excise it. Although we can never succeed in doing this, even the attempt to do it will leave us fragmented and no longer whole. This attitude toward sexuality has been quite common in many periods of history and it is often found today, in two apparently contradictory forms. The first form is that of the sexual ascetic, who is repelled by sex and is determined to live as a non-sexed being. The sexual ascetic is disgusted by sex and rejects it, thereby denying a fundamental structure of his/her personality. This always has serious consequences. (Note carefully that such "asceticism" has nothing to do with the decision to remain unmarried for the sake of the kingdom—that is, to enter religious life in the religious orders which are found in the Catholic church and in some Protestant churches. It is possible to find sexual ascetics, in the negative sense in which I use the term here, in religious life, but it is my impression that there are not many. In fact, they seem to be much more common outside religious life, and they are frequently found even among the unchurched.)

There is a second way in which we may try to separate ourselves from our sexuality. Years ago, it would have been called the approach of the libertine. Today it is often called sexual freedom, but it could be better described as the playboy or playgirl approach. The sole concern of those who practice it is to maximize copulation while avoiding all personal involvement. This Guinness-Book-of-Records approach to sexuality is usually found, not in those who are at peace with their sexual powers, but in those who doubt them. (Not that they doubt their physical powers; what they doubt, often with reason, is that these physical powers are the expression of a deep and authentic manliness or womanliness.) Those plagued by such doubts often try to mask them by living up to the popular image of the sexual athlete (above all, by talking incessantly and irresponsibly about their prowess), and by viewing the ideal man or woman as one whose desire is equalled only by his/her stamina, but who is never touched personally by his/her "loves." It may seem paradoxical, but this second approach is also motivated by contempt for sex. We strip sexuality of its personal dimension because we fear it; and we fear it because we feel that anything which is deeply embedded within our personality, while eluding our attempts to cope with it, is a threat to our autonomy and our integrity. The attitude of the sexual athlete toward sex is just as negative as that of the sexual ascetic, although his approach is superficially different. His motto is "I can have it, but I can remain untarnished by it, because it has nothing whatsoever to do with the real me."

Our Bodies: Ourselves

It is dangerous to try to separate ourselves from our sexuality, and the dangers involved are all rooted in one fact: the body is not a *part* of the person, of the self. The body is not the lower part of our nature and it is not the source of our sinful tendencies. The human ideal is not to subject the body to the soul. The truth is very different: the body is the revelation of the person and the symbol of personal presence and engagement. It is in and through the body that we can be present in a definite time and place. It is in the body that we achieve our full human reality.

This brings us to a point hinted at above. For human beings, both love and hate, both authentic existence and its opposite, become definitively real and become historical fact, only when they find bodily expression. Because our sexuality is total, because it touches the very center of our personal existence, its final realization in the body will manifest all that a person is, for good or for evil. Both the mature and balanced personality as well as the warped and twisted personality will be revealed here. But it is important to see that the warping and twisting will appear, not because there is something inherently questionable or evil about bodily sexuality, but because physical sexuality is the revelation of all that we are; it is the revelation of our *selves*. Confusion about this is the source of at least some of the taboos associated with sex, and this confusion is probably behind the so-called "vestal principle"—the notion that those who function in religious ceremonies should be without sexual experience or should have abstained for some period of time.

The fact that our sexuality is total implies that it is not good practice to refer to our sexual powers and actions as the "animal" part of our nature, as though it were precisely here that our kinship with the rest of the animal world were manifest. It seems clear that in important respects we human beings are far more profoundly "sexed" than the other animals, and that we are far more deeply conditioned by this orientation to our polar opposites, to members of the opposite sex. One indication of this is the fact that fertility and the desire for sexual activity are not limited to certain periods among human beings, as they are in the case of the other animals. (A number of palaeoanthropologists feel that the development of year-round sexual desire and availability was a vital factor in the evolutionary success of primitive human beings.)[17]

A Polarity Vital in All Areas

Because sexuality is total, it touches all of the dimensions of our lives—emotion, intelligence, thought, and action. Sexual polarization is vital in all areas; and in all of them, men and women have distinct and equally important contributions to make. This principle (the *distinctiveness* of the contributions of men and women), although sound in itself, has often led to the exclusion of women from some sectors of life, on the grounds that they were not intelligent or not capable of being educated; and this, in turn, has often led to the exploitation of women. Here again, there are serious problems with the so-called "Christian" tradition, and the matter is important enough to justify a brief glance at some of the elements of this tradition.

The Christian Tradition and the Role of Women

Thomas Aquinas' attitudes on this question are interesting in themselves, and they are important because of the great influence he had on the whole later Catholic tradition. Writing in his *Summa Theologiae*, he asserted that "Good order would have been wanting in the family if some were not governed by those wiser than themselves. So, by such a kind of subjection, woman is naturally subject to man, because in man, the power of reason predominates."[18] Earlier in the same article, Thomas had affirmed that "It was necessary for woman to be made as a helpmate for man; not, indeed, as some maintain, as a help in any other work, for in any other work, a man can be more suitably helped by another man, but precisely for having children."[19] (These citations do not discredit Thomas or his theology, because, in them, Thomas was simply echoing the views of his own day and age, the "common nonsense" of the period in which he lived. What these citations do show is the degree to which even a brilliant mind can fail to think critically when the influence of social and cultural factors is strong enough.)

In the tradition which derived from Thomas, it was usually implied that women were not capable of clear and critical thought, and that they were perhaps not entirely rational; and in some respects, this tradition has endured to our own day. A number of Catholic books about marriage, written in the last forty or fifty years, were strongly influenced by some similar views of Pius XI, in his Encyclical, *Casti Connubii*, published in 1930.[20]

The real problem with such views is this: if women are treated as though they are deficient in intelligence and in the power of critical thought, then we will be faced with a classic form of the self-fulfilling prophecy; women treated in this way will act accordingly, to the immense disadvantage of *both men and women*. In the ordinary course of events, men become fully men only in the polar relationship with women; and when the image of women, as an ideal or in fact, is distorted, it is men who suffer the greatest harm. The man who fears an intelligent and competent woman is one who has profound doubts about his manhood—a fact which he often attempts to disguise, even from himself, by various "macho" antics and poses.

The interesting question of the origin of such attitudes is one which we can touch on only briefly, and it is a question on which there is really not much agreement. A number of anthropologists feel that during most of the tenure of prehistoric man on earth, society was matriarchical, and that the shift to patriarchical patterns came only with the introduction of agriculture, with its more settled way of life. According to this theory, male domination is the result of a long and bitter struggle on the part of men to overthrow an earlier phase of female dominance. This is rather speculative and does not really explain much, although it is true that there were certain negative factors at work in the rise of towns and cities which could lead to the subjugation of women. One fact which is worth noting, although it is not easy to explain, is the general deterioration of the status of women in the Greco-Roman world during the first millenium B.C., and in Israelite-Jewish society, beginning about five hundred years earlier. There were some striking exceptions, of course. There is every indication that in Etruscan society, women enjoyed virtual equality with men in all important areas, and this may also have been the case in Cretan society of the late second millenium B.C.; it is unfortunate that we know next to nothing about the cultural factors which brought this about.

The evidence on these questions, historical and psychological, is by no means complete, but perhaps this can be said: for reasons which we will discuss later in the book, sexuality appears to be more pervasive in the life of the woman than it is in the life of the man. A woman is in more peaceful possession of her sexuality and has an easier and more natural relationship to it than does a man. Since sex is a domain of ecstasy and mystery, of receptivity and spontaneity, a society which aims at the control and subjugation of nature, and which sees knowledge primarily in terms of the adaptation of means to given ends, will manifest considerable hostility toward those elements in it which pose a threat to its goals. A society which confuses intelligence with reason is annoyed by mystery and threatened by the ecstatic side of life. During the periods mentioned above, Israelite-Jewish society, as well as the culture of the Greco-Roman world began in some significant ways to regard the rational control of life as an ideal, and, for the reasons suggested, women may have suffered because of this. (On the other hand, the view that is espoused by some radical feminists today—namely that there is a profound and primordial hostility between the sexes, or that men, by nature, need to and want to dominate women—is ideological nonsense, and the "evidence" for it does not come from the normal human situation but from pathological distortions of that situation.)

A Creative Tension

Because our sexuality touches every aspect of the personality, there are distinctive manly and womanly ways of understanding, feeling, and acting; there are distinctive manly and womanly forms of imagination, reason, and decision. A naive misunderstanding of this fact has led in the past to the absurd judgment that women cannot reason and that men must not have feelings; but this misunderstanding cannot be removed by attempting to level the distinctions between the sexes, or to minimize their differences, or to pretend that they are all the result of social conditioning. The polarity of man and woman is essential in all areas of life. It is essential in our business and professional lives, in research, in the arts and in government, in the personal and communal search for justice, and it is essential in the area of the human being's relation with God—that is, in religion, and in worship. When women are systematically excluded from key positions in any of these areas, the human community suffers and each of us suffers as an individual. Much of the vitality, the charm, and the very humanity of life comes from the creative tension which should always be present in every encounter between men and women.

If we felt the need to express this in the literary form of the bumper sticker, we might put it this way: *The sexualization of life is the humanization of life.* Like most bumper sticker philosophy, this needs considerable elaboration before it makes sense, but this is precisely what we must do here. The sexualization of life (which must be sharply distinguished from the incessant babbling about sex which is so common today) is a good and necessary thing, precisely because human sexuality cannot be confined to the biological realm. Life in its entirety is sexual;

thought, imagery, and motivation, our perception of value and our response to it, are all conditioned by the fact that we exist as either men or women. This fact, that human life is sexual in its entirety, was clearly seen by Sigmund Freud (though perhaps to some degree misinterpreted by him because of a puritanical streak in his nature) and bitterly resisted by many of his contemporaries, who, like many people at all stages of history, regarded sex as ignoble and animalistic, if not positively evil.

The authentic sexualization of life (something we should desire and work for) comes about when the polarity and the creative tension of the encounter between the sexes is found and is fostered in all sectors of life. It occurs when the sexes are totally equal, totally different, and therefore *totally complementary*.

Note carefully that to say that our thought and imagination are sexual is not the same thing as saying that we fantasize about sex all of the time (though this is probably the case more often than we care to admit). Our thought and imagination are sexual, not only in their *object,* but in their very nature. The symbols and images without which we cannot think are sexually conditioned and of sexual provenance and origin. These sexual symbols are present in all forms of art and are given reflective expression in literature. Men and women who are artists use sexual symbols differently, and these symbols exert a different evocative power on men and women. In this connection it is interesting to note the unabashed and unembarrassed sexual imagery of the Old Testament: the sexual relationship between man and woman is used as the symbol and analog for the relationship of the human being with God (particularly in the works of Hosea and Isaiah and in the Song of Songs).

This sexual conditioning of the imagination has some consequences which might interest the philosophically minded reader. If the imagination, the symbol-making power, is sexually conditioned, and therefore qualitatively different in men and women, then a careful reading of what Thomas Aquinas has to say about the relationship of intelligence and the imagination would indicate that this qualitative distinction extends into the realm of understanding as well.[21] In the text cited, Thomas asks an interesting question: he asks whether, in the process of understanding, we find intelligibility, intelligible content, in a world of its own, or *in* the product of our imaginative faculties. Thomas insists that the latter is the case, because the proper object of human intelligence is not the pure idea, but the idea *embodied* in matter, where it is capable of affecting our senses. The consequences are fascinating.

It is extremely important to distinguish the authentic sexualization of life from the utilization of sex which is so common today. The sexualization of life has nothing to do with the prevalence of talk about sex, with which we are glutted; in the proper sense of the word, we are not really living in a sexualized society today. Sex is exploited for commercial purposes, and it is used to sell everything from soap and deodorants to cars and condominiums. But the problem is precisely that: sex is being *used*. However, our sexuality belongs to the personal sphere of life, and to *use* persons or personal goods is wrong. This use of sex runs the gamut from the carefully calculated "jiggle" in the TV commercial, through the adolescent humor apparently favored by those who determine the Nielson ratings. It runs from the titillating blurbs for TV mini-series and magazine stories, all the way to hard-core pornography and the use of call-girls in the business world. We live in a world of incessant sexual stimuli, but this has nothing to do with the authentic sexualization of life. Such stimuli cater to the voyeur in all of us, but they do not express the creative tension of man and woman, and they do not summon us to realize and achieve that creative tension in our lives. In the midst of the omnipresent sexual stimuli of the entertainment and commercial worlds, our society is pitifully *undersexualized*.

What can be done about this? We can begin by observing that one of the principal functions of art, in all of its forms, is to bring about this authentic sexualization of life, and that the art of any period can be judged by its success or failure in this respect. This is true both of serious and popular art, and a few examples will illustrate the point. The novels of the Norwegian author Sigrid Undset (both the medieval trilogies and tetralogies as well as her works which have a modern setting) are a profound and beautiful statement of the relationship between the sexes—a relationship which has moments of grandeur and moments of tragedy, but without which human life would be unbearably dull. On the level of serious drama, the Burton/Taylor version of the *Taming of the Shrew* is a masterpiece of comedy which succeeds in making a profound statement about the creative tension of the relationship of man and woman. On a more popular level, the most memorable movies of every period are absorbing for their treatment of the polarity between the sexes and for their revelation of the creative and transforming power which this polarity can unleash. Reflect, too, on the fascination which the human body has always had for sculpture and pictorial art. Genuine art never uses sex to sell itself; it respects and esteems human sexuality and is fascinated and intrigued by it. Genuine art uses sexual imagery to depict the human ideal, and it is in this way that art promotes the sexualization of life.

Sexuality and Identity

There is another very important consequence of the fact that human sexuality is total and is not merely a part or function of the personality: accepting and affirming our sexuality is the way to full and authentic personhood. (Note carefully that this is not the same as saying that we cannot be persons without frequent or periodic intercourse, or without engaging in a full sexual relationship on all levels of our existence. The point which is being made here is this: we must affirm and accept ourselves *as* men or women, and we must be at peace with this fact. Furthermore, to affirm ourselves as men is to affirm and accept our dependence on women and to affirm ourselves as women is to affirm and accept our dependence on men.)

Karl Barth expressed this very well in volume three of his *Church Dogmatics:* "The human being cannot be really human before God and other human beings, except by defining himself as man in terms of woman, or defining herself as woman in terms of man. This created, physiological characteristic which the human being possesses in common with the animals, by no means represents the animal element in human beings, but constitutes our most fundamental characteristic."[22] Note, of course, that this "defining" of which Barth speaks, will vary with the different periods of life and that it touches all of our human relationships, and not merely the sexual relationship in the narrow sense. For example, the parent of the opposite sex offers the child the opportunity to define him/herself in terms of the opposite sex, and brothers and sisters do this for one another in a different way. Acquaintances and friends of the opposite sex also fulfill this role, not only during the period of dating, but throughout our lives. This dependence of man and woman on each other does not exclude an authentic celibate vocation, but it does demand that, in some form, dialogue with the other sex be allowed to play its proper role during the formative years of those who are given such a vocation. No matter what our walk in life, unless we accept our manhood or womanhood as conditioning us as *persons,* and therefore as involving us in a polar relationship with that other form of personhood represented by the opposite sex, our achievement of human personality will be stunted and limited.

The Love Which Defines Us as Persons

Since our sexuality is total and personal, to become a person in the full sense of the word is to become man or woman, with all that that implies. But to be a person is to be able to love, to be there for another; and this means that to be a person is to be capable of a distinctly manly or womanly love. The love which defines us as persons is precisely this distinctively manly or womanly love, and it is, in this sense of the word, sexual.

This love comes into being in our earliest years and it grows in all of those relationships which reflect the complementarity of the sexes. It is true that there is a certain ambiguity about the term "sexual love" which might make us uneasy in using it to describe a relationship in which physical or genital sexuality should play no role—for example, the relationships of parents with children of the opposite sex, brothers and sisters with each other. The term "sexual love" is often restricted to genital expressions of sexual love, that is, to sexual intercourse and to all forms of behavior which lead, of themselves, to sexual intercourse. But the term can be used in a more general sense to refer to any and every human love which derives its special character from the fact that it is a real love and it involves those of opposite sex.

It is not particularly important that all of these forms of love be called "sexual," but it is extremely important to recognize the sexual component in parental love, in the love of brothers and sisters, and in the love of friends of the opposite sex, who, by reason of age or other factors, would never be thought of as partners in a genital sexual relationship. And it is very important that we be comfortable with the sexual character of these relationships, because it is precisely this aspect which plays such an important role in leading us to psycho-sexual maturity. These relationships confront us with the human reality of the opposite sex, without which we can neither define ourselves nor develop that clear sexual identity which is essential for authentic personhood.

This means that the achievement of an authentic manly or womanly love is a task of central importance for all: for the not-yet-married, for those who are married, for those who, by reason of circumstances or personal choice, will never marry. It also means that for those who have chosen marriage, the specific form of manly or womanly love which is proper to this state of life—namely conjugal or sexual love in the full sense—is a way of achieving the human ideal to which they are called.

3.

The Challenge of Human

Sexuality

Our sexuality extends to all levels and dimensions of our personal being, and it is precisely as persons that we are sexual. Because of this our sexuality is not simply a *given,* a datum of existence, but is rather a *challenge* and, when it is what it should be, an *achievement.*

Personal Existence as a Vocation

Sexuality is a personal value, and, like other personal values, it is something which we are called on to achieve. The personal dignity and worth which we have, even before we are born, belong to us precisely because of what we can become—namely persons in the full sense of the word, who can know and love, who can be known and be loved. We are called to be persons, and therefore, personhood in the full sense is our vocation. As persons, we are ends and goals in ourselves, and never mere means. Persons have value in themselves, and they are never to be valued merely for their usefulness in attaining some other end. The summons to become a person is the summons to live and act as one who has infinite value, and to be a self who can be given to another without in any way being diminished or lost. This call to become a "self," a person, is simply the call to achieve wholeness and integration by striving to unify all levels and dimensions of our being and it is the call to personalize them by making them part of a human existence which is *for others*.

The Nature of the Task: Integration

This integration of all the elements of our lives, this attempt to make them part of personal existence, is the fundamental human challenge, even apart from the question of sexuality. It is the challenge which we face in the world of work and of business, and it applies to our attitudes toward money and property and toward food and drink. In all of these areas, our task is to personalize these sectors of our lives and to make sure that they serve and promote the good of the person.

But integrating sexuality into a truly personal existence is the greatest challenge and it is one which we cannot avoid, because for each of us existence itself is that of man or woman. Each of us, in existing as man or woman, is powerfully drawn to the opposite sex, intellectually, emotionally, and physically. This fact of our personal existence is not a limitation of our freedom; rather, it is a very important part of the total situation in which our freedom is to be achieved. There is no pure "I" behind or underneath the concrete conditions of my life—an "I" which would have to tolerate these conditions, but for which these conditions would constitute, in the final analysis, obstacles to be removed or avoided. These conditions, and most prominent among them is the fact that we exist as sexed beings, either men or women, constitute the field in which we are called to move from being potential persons to being actual persons or, in other words, to become men and women who actually know and love others. Our vocation is to achieve personhood, to love with a truly human love, and this means to love *as sexed beings* and not apart from or aside from this most fundamental characteristic of our personal existence. (We should draw attention here to the definition of "person" which is assumed in this discussion: a person is one whose existence for him/herself is identical with his/her existence for another. A person, in the full sense of the word, is one who has grasped the essential mystery of being: that to *be,* fully and unrestrictedly, is to be *for* another. This is the meaning of the statement in John's Gospel that God is love.)

The Moral Imperative for Human Sexuality

To accept the challenge of integrating our sexuality is to accept all of the structures of our manhood or womanhood and to do all we can to insure that they serve authentic love—that is, our power to be there for the other (and in some way, through this "other," for *all* others). There is a basic moral imperative which is consequent on this: we ought to accept our manhood or womanhood honestly and joyfully. We ought to accept it both as fact and as gift, and we ought always ask just one question: how can the physiological, psychological, emotional, and spiritual structures of our manhood or womanhood symbolize, manifest, and effect authentic love, and not one of the many counterfeit versions or parodies of love. There is only one real moral imperative for our sexuality: that it be informed by genuine love. This programmatic statement is easy to make and exceedingly difficult to implement. Sex *can* easily become self-centered, and in doing so it will destroy personal values. But we must never lose sight of the fact that such failures are due to the absence of authentic love and not to the failure to subordinate sex to some other goal.

The basic moral imperative for our sexuality is rooted in the fact that we are not called to be angels but to be men and women—human beings who are animals, but who stand out above the animal world because of our power to make and use symbols, and to endow the physical, material world with meaning. Ideally, when man and woman express themselves sexually to each other, their love-making is a sign of their desire to find the center and meaning of their own existence in each other. The moral task is not to bring this love-making under "control," by limiting it as much as possible, but rather to do all in our power to make sexual union a profound form of "being there" for the other.[23]

The Non-Identity of Love and Sexual Expression

To talk about the integration of our sexuality as a challenge is to emphasize that our sexuality is not naturally integrated. Integration of our sexuality is a possibility, but so is disintegration. We can be, and often are, selfish and self-centered in this area of life, as well as in others; we do not have to be. The integration of sexuality is a challenge because love, on the one hand, and the physical expression of our sexuality, on the other, are not the same, not identical. Perhaps more than any other facet of our personalities, this is the source of our grandeur and tragedy as human beings. Our sexual behavior symbolizes and realizes all that we are and it is for this reason that it manifests both the depth and genuineness of our love as well as our deficiencies and failures in loving. A sexual relationship does not leave the partners untouched, because our attempts to make love reveal our true feelings toward each other (even when we attempt to hide these feelings from each other and from ourselves). The sexual relationship ideally is an expression of our love and our trust, and it is a state in which we find security and joy and peace. But the sexual relationship often falls short of the ideal; it may be the expression of fear and even of hatred, and we may find in it only anxiety and inner turmoil. Facile optimism about sex is just as ungrounded as is the cynical pessimism which sees sex as basically selfish and self-centered.[24]

Love and Sex: Sexual Love

This leads to a critically important insight: love and sexual expression *can* fuse and merge, and their union is one very high form of the integration of sexuality. It is also a moral ideal and a good which should be whole-heartedly sought. (In this section, when we speak of "sexual expression," we are speaking of genital sexual behavior—that is, sexual intercourse, and other physical expressions of sexuality which ordinarily lead to intercourse or are associated with it.) The fusion of love and sexual expression could be called simply *sexual love*, although this can lead to confusion because this term is often misused as a synonym for sexual intercourse. This *is* a misuse because intercourse can occur without love, and "sexual love" should clearly not mean "sexual expression without love." Sexual expression apart from true sexual love is a serious distortion of human sexuality, and, in the final analysis, it represents our only real failure as sexed beings.

Less obviously, but no less seriously, sexual love is not love plus sex or sex plus love. Such expressions assume that, in themselves, love and sexual expression do not have much to do with each other, although they can be united, pulled together. But such an approach does not do justice to the unity of sexual love, or to the inner need and demand of our sexuality to be fulfilled in love. Sexual love is a complex unity which can be understood only with the help of the personal categories of knowing and loving. It is an act (and even more an attitude) which embodies these values and makes them incarnate in a unique way in the here and now. Human love is not an abstraction; it is not disembodied and it is not purely spiritual. The love which we need is truly human, at once a physical and a psychological reality.[25]

The biological and physical elements of this love should not be separated from this love in its entirety. When the spiritual and the physical merge in sexual love, something new is created which is more than the sum of the disparate elements. Something specifically human has happened: matter has become the bearer of spiritual value, and spirit has become embodied in matter; matter has been transformed, and spirit has been given concreteness and life.

In his fine book, *Motivation and Personality*, Abraham Maslow discussed the merging and fusion of love and sexual expression. He discussed it not precisely as a moral ideal (which is the point we are making here) but rather as the manifestation of the healthy or, as he called it, the "self-actualizing" personality. However, his conclusions have very important moral implications.

Maslow pointed out that the sex-life of psychologically healthy people is quite distinctive, and he was confident that if we attempt to describe it carefully, we can draw some very accurate conclusions about the nature of love. In his interviews with happily married people, he found that love and the physical expression of sex were very frequently joined or fused. Maslow was quite aware that love and sexual expression were conceptually distinct, but at the same time he noted that in the lives of healthy people they tended to become less separate, and that they even tended to merge. Maslow was even tempted to suggest that any person who is capable of sexual pleasure without genuine love, is sick (although he stopped just short of saying it!); but he does affirm that psychologically healthy people will not seek sexual expression for its own sake, and they will never be satisfied by it, unless it is part of love.[26]

Studies by other psychologists and psychiatrists seem to support Maslow's conclusions. Oswald Schwarz spoke for many in his profession when he noted that love and what he called "sexual impulse" are fundamentally different, but he also found that in the fully mature human being, they cannot be found in isolation. He even called this insight "the fundamental principle of any psychology of sex."[27]

Fusion without Confusion

However, when love and sexual expression merge to form a new unity—sexual love—they do so without becoming confused with each other and without becoming identified. Sexual expression is, ideally, a way of achieving love, and it becomes something on which love builds. It becomes more and more fully integrated into love, and it becomes less sought for its own sake and in isolation. This fact, that love and sexual expression are not the same, is very important for understanding the celibate vocation, that is, the vocation of those who are called to religious life and who remain unmarried "for the sake of the kingdom."

If love and sexual expression were identified, then the distinctively manly or womanly love which is available to us as human beings would not be possible outside of a conjugal, marriage-like situation. If they are not identified, then real psycho-sexual maturity is possible for those who choose a way of life which does not involve genital sexual expression.

However, this non-identity of love and sex is also extremely important for understanding the way in which love and sexuality are related in sexual love itself. Discussing the relationship between love and sexual expression, Maslow drew attention to some paradoxes which he found quite intriguing. He had a very strong impression that sexual pleasures were found in their most intense and ecstatic perfection in self-actualizing people; and yet, their attitude toward the orgasm was quite different from that which he had observed in less psychologically healthy people. He found that for those whom he called "self-actualizing," the orgasm was a profound and ecstatic experience, but he also found that these people were not *dependent* on the orgasm, not obsessed with it, as were others. He noted that they could accept the absence of sexual expression with equanimity, even though, when it was given them, they enjoyed it more than others. He summarized his clinical experience by observing that psychologically healthy people do not need sensuality to the degree that others do, but that enjoy it far more deeply when it is present.[28]

Paul Tillich, probably the best-known American theologian from the mid-thirties until his death in 1965, discussed the same question from a more theoretical point of view but came to very similar conclusions. Tillich argued that pleasure is present in or results from the creative act, but that if the act is intended as a means of attaining pleasure, then at that moment creativity comes to an end. Moreover, as soon as we begin to reflect on the pleasurable consequences of our actions, that deeply human joy which is a concomitant of the truly creative act, ceases to exist. According to Tillich, the pain/pleasure principle (that is, acting simply in order to avoid pain or to procure pleasure) is valid only in those who are not psychologically healthy and therefore not truly free.[29]

This point is essential for understanding human sexuality, and it could be summarized in this way: ideally, human sexuality and sexual expression are taken up into love and enveloped by it. Human sexual expression points beyond itself, and when its inner dynamisms are realized (in both senses: "known" and "made real"), at that very moment sexual expression finds its true identity and meaning. Paradoxically, it is affirmed and transcended at the same time. But at the moment at which it is transcended, it is not lost, but rather found again: it has become a sign and expression of love and its vital dynamisms have been put at the service of love. Sexual pleasure is no longer something to be sought for itself, but neither will it be despised and rejected in the name of a false asceticism.

The Tension between Love and Sexual Expression

This tension is the key to the mystery of sexuality. The fusion of love and sexual expression remains a challenge, and it is one of the most important moral tasks which the overwhelming majority of human beings have to face. Those who followed Freud and developed his insights have sometimes been slow to realize this, because of a peculiarity in Freud's own thought. Despite his undoubted achievements in pointing out the total character of human sexuality, he tended to derive love from sex or to confuse the two, which was a bad mistake. It is their non-identity and the tension between love and sexual expression which makes their fusion a challenge which summons the best energies and efforts of the human being.

Listing Some Preliminary Insights

This would be an appropriate place to list some insights about human sexuality which appear in the work, both of thoughtful psychiatrists and of theologians. These insights will provide us with valuable guidelines when we turn, in the fourth chapter, to the complex unity of sexual love.

Human Sexuality Is Unique

There is nothing in the world quite like human sexuality. It has its own goals and purposes, and therefore it possesses dynamisms (tendencies to achieve those purposes) which are unique and proper to itself. Sexuality plays a role in human life which is quite different from that played by sexual differentiation in the life of any other animal. It is a deep misunderstanding to view our sexuality as something which we share with the other animals, and therefore as something "animalistic" in the pejorative sense. This is a distorted view and it has done great harm.

Human beings have a sex instinct only in a very improper sense of the latter word; in fact, in normal human beings, sexuality is so complex and involves so many elements which are absent from the sexual activity of the other animals, that a purely biological theory of instincts is utterly unable to account for them. Sensuality or sensual pleasure owes much more to psychological factors than to purely physical ones, and this shows how absurd it is to regard sensual pleasure as an "animal" phenomenon. [30] (This view runs counter to an attitude which has been prevalent in some Catholic writings on sexuality until very recent times—an attitude which regards sexuality as "bestial" unless restrained or justified by some other motive, usually procreation.)

Sexuality and Communication

A second insight into human sexuality is equally important: the relationship of love to sexual expression suggests that *communion* and *communication* would be good categories to use for understanding human sexuality. When sexual expression is what it should be, it is an act of knowing and it is the experience of being known. It is the speaking of a word and the hearkening to a word—a word whose creative possibilities touch all of the dimensions of the lives of the man and the woman involved. Human sexual love is an act of deep, personal, existential knowledge, and therefore it is an act of being present to and in communion with another. When a man and woman love each other, what they really intend is to share the total life and destiny of each other, and they tend to regard sexual union as a way of bringing about and expressing this existential communion.

True Sexual Freedom

The integration of sexual expression in love has a liberating effect on our sexuality. This is a true liberation and has nothing to do with promiscuity or with casual "sex for fun," practiced with a variety of partners. When sexual expression is integrated into love and is an expression of love, then it becomes possible for us to accept our manhood or womanhood in all of its dimensions in a simple and healthy way. Then we can accept the fact that we are sexually attracted to those of the opposite sex, without feeling the need to let such attraction develop into a sexual relationship (in the genital sense). To put it simply, the greater the fusion between love and sexual expression in marriage, the less the need to engage in what are basically neurotic extra-marital adventures.[31] It seems clear from this that much of what is called "sexual freedom" today, and much of the "liberation" which the sixties brought is nothing more than neurotic and often infantile behavior.

4.

The Fusion of Love and Sexual Expression: Sexual Love

A Question of Terminology

This would be an appropriate place to define some terms and to adopt a slightly different (but more accurate) definition of the term "sexual love." We will use the term "sexual love" primarily in speaking of a state or situation in which two persons exist, and in virtue of which they can act in a characteristic way. The term, as we use it, will refer indirectly to sexual intercourse, in so far as this act *can* be the fulfillment and the realization, at one point in time, of the state of being sexually in love with this other person. What we call "sexual love" is often called "conjugal" or "marital" love (the first of these is from the Latin *conjunx,* spouse). These terms are acceptable enough, provided that sexual love, as we will describe it, is seen as the ideal which marriage strives to attain. They are not acceptable if they imply that sexual love is usually, or obviously attained in marriage and never outside of the institution. As we will see in a later section of this book the real justification of marriage, its deepest *raison d'être*, is its suitability for the attainment of sexual love, *if* this latter term is understood in the right way.

Our purpose is to understand sexual love. And we are seeking an understanding which does not remain in the realm of theory, but leads to a great esteem for sexual love, and which, for most people, should lead to the responsible attempt to achieve sexual love in a permanent and stable relationship. Understanding always implies the perception of unity, and although sexual love touches many different aspects of human existence, we will try to understand how they are taken up into the multi-dimensional unity of sexual love. Our approach will be to describe the state of mind and heart of a man and a woman who have this kind of love for each other.

Note carefully that the understanding which we seek has nothing to do with the "mastery" of sexual love, as though, having mastered the theory, one could, in some automatic way, achieve it in one's life. Sexual love is always a gift, but it is a gift of which we may remain largely unaware if we are not attentive, and it is a gift to which we may fail to respond if we do not understand it. The understanding of sexual love which we seek here is not the work of technical reason, which chooses suitable means to attain given ends. It is rather that most fundamental act of understanding which consists in being open to the charm and beauty of reality and in striving to respond to it.

An Ambiguous Term?

There is an obvious problem with the term "sexual love," which we alluded to in the previous section. The term is often used as a synonym for sexual intercourse, which may, at times, be an expression of sexual love, but which may, in other circumstances, have nothing to do with sexual love. But despite the ambiguity, the term "sexual love" is well-suited to describe that love of a man and a woman for each other, which they give and receive in a distinctively manly and womanly way, and which touches and transforms all aspects of their personal being.

I prefer the term "sexual love" for two reasons. Real love is always a rarity, although parodies of love abound. Sexual love is very rare, too. It is a marvelous love, but it is also a threatened love, and one of the most dangerous threats to which it has been exposed in some religious traditions is the desire and the attempt to control it, limit it, and, in that way, to "spiritualize" it. As we have seen, these attempts seem to be motivated by the fear that if sexual love becomes too sexual, it will lose the purity of true love and degenerate into egoism and sensuality. Against such attempts, the *sexual* character of this love must be maintained.

There is a second reason for preferring the term "sexual love": this love is also threatened by attempts to dissolve it into chemistry or physiology, or to see in it simply the discharge of accumulated tension. Against such attempts, it must be maintained that sexual love is *love*—the effective, willed commitment of this man to this woman, this woman to this man.

This marvelous and threatened love is totally human. It has a flesh and blood reality which makes benevolence and sympathy seem pale and wan by comparison. But at the same time it is inspired by an idealism and a concern for the other which make infatuation and the mere release of sexual energy seem to be nothing more than a tragic fragmenting of the personality, if they are separated from this concern. The word "love" should be used sparingly, with a certain reserve and reticence. Love can never really be talked *about*, in the sense that we could make it into an object, to be subjected to cool and dispassionate examination. Love can only be reflected on from *within*, and such reflection is the attempt to become more consciously present to the mystery which one has received and which one is living. But such reflection is good, and it serves love, because love which is consciously present to its own mystery is more true to itself and more fully verifies the definition of love.

Sexual Love as a Total Personal Response

Sexual love, as we use the term here, could be described this way: *it is the total personal response of this man to this woman, of this woman to this man.* This response can be thought of, first, as a deep and powerful feeling, provided that this word "feeling" is defined as we have already defined "emotion"—that is, as an act of understanding which is sensitive to the charm and beauty of what is understood. Taken in this sense, the word "feeling" is good, because it expresses the fact that sexual love is a unity of flesh and blood, mind and spirit.

Sexual love is clearly a feeling of a special kind, belonging with those human feelings which can be called "other directed." It is not self-contained (as, for example, are hunger, and thirst, and sexual tension). It is a feeling which does not have its term and center in the one who experiences it, but rather in another. It is a feeling which *intends* (reaches out toward) the other, and in virtue of which one is drawn to him/her. In this respect it resembles the feelings of awe and wonder, but these feelings can be inspired by the mystery inherent in *things*, whereas the feeling of sexual love is the experience of being drawn by the mystery unique to this woman, this man. The other person is seen as an end or goal in her/himself. The other is never primarily (and really never at all) a means to attain something for oneself.

The Transcendence of Time

Sexual love is a *personal* response because it is a way of "being there," of existing, for the other as a person. It is the gift of self to one who can know and love; it is a gift which is confident of what the other can become, under the creative power of such a love; and therefore, it is the implicit request for that same gift of self on the part of the loved one. Because true sexual love is concerned about the other as a person, it wants and affirms that transcendence of time which is an aspect of our personal being. Only a person really has a past and a future. Personal existence has a kind of eternity about it, touching and enveloping the three modes of time, without being confined to any one of them. Sexual love sees the future as a mode of greater and greater fulfillment for this relationship with the loved one, and for this reason, it is *essentially a permanent commitment*. In the concrete, sexual love does fall short of this ideal—in fact it does so quite often—but it is important to note that when it does, this happens, not because of the absence of some additional quality (such as "control" or some other justifying motive) but rather because sexual love in a given case is simply not "loving" enough, and has somehow failed to be a way of "being there" fully and unrestrictedly for the other.

Sexual Love and Union

Sexual love is a total personal response which wants and craves union with the other, and this union is seen, by those who are in love, as something right and proper and good. This union is certainly sexual, in the narrower sense of the word (that is, in the sense of genital sexuality). However, it is not only this, but it touches life in its entirety: we want to be with this other person, close to her/him, sharing as much of her/his life as possible.

At its deepest level, this union is a *knowing* of this other person and a real act of acceptance of her/him. Knowledge and understanding always involve a union of the separated, a moving out toward another and a union with the other. Further, to the degree to which the self and the other merge, the self-affirmation which is a necessary part of our own reality reaches out to include and envelop the other person. This is the thought expressed so beautifully in the New Testament by the author of the *Epistle to the Ephesians* 5:28-32.[32]

Those interested in probing the thought more deeply might want to reflect again on the words of Thomas Aquinas in his *Summa Theologiae* I, 84, 7. Thomas asserts there that human understanding is the work of the intellect (a spiritual power), functioning in conjunction with the bodily faculties of sensation. This thought could be developed in a way which would see sexual love, in the sense in which that term is being used here, as one of the the most fully human forms of knowing available to the intelligent animal. (And recall, in this connection, the Old Testament's use of the Hebrew verb for "know" as a synonym of sexual intercourse.) [33]

The knowledge and acceptance which are spoken of here are the very heart and essence of sexual love, but it is important to note that the physical, bodily, sensitive, and sensual elements are not transcended in the sense of being left behind or of becoming in some way dispensable. These elements remain the indispensable substratum, the "body" of love, in and through which the very essence of love is realized and manifested and made incarnate. The deep understanding and acceptance which are the fullness of sexual love are never elements which are simply added to our sexuality or merely juxtaposed with it, and they certainly are not in conflict with it. They are the fulfillment of sexuality, occurring at the moment and in the measure in which sexuality has come to be what it really should be.

The Signs of Sexual Love

Sexual love is a feeling which absorbs our attention. It does not occur at the periphery of the personality, but it touches the center of our personal lives and engages us in our totality as persons. Sexual love awakens within us a whole range of feelings which are themselves facets of human fulfillment, but which are not sought in and for themselves: enjoyment, elation, ecstasy. In sexual love, the focus is always on the other person and not on our own feelings. We intend the other and not ourselves or some aspect of our emotional lives. (Recall, in this connection, Paul Tillich's remarks about the pleasure/pain principle and the role it plays in the uncreative and sick personality.)[34]

Sexual love absorbs our attention in the sense that we want to be with the loved person in as many ways as possible, to share her/his life as fully as can be, in thought and in activity, in joy and in sorrow. A major element in such love is physical closeness and intimacy, and it is precisely in this light that sexual intimacy (in the sense of genital sexuality) is understood by a man and a woman who are deeply in love. They want to be *with* and *for* each other, and their being together is a source of unending delight.

The Element of Play

The tenderness and affection of sexual love is clearly a manifestation of caring for this other person, of assuming responsibility for her/him, and of wanting to foster and promote her/his life as far as is in our power. But Maslow mentioned another element which came to the fore in the interviews he conducted with self-actualizing people and which clearly has much to do with the fact that sexual love absorbs our attention. He found that Fromm and Adler, who have rightly stressed productivity, care, and responsibility in the healthy love relationship, were a bit over-serious, and strangely omitted one very important aspect of the healthy love relationship: fun, merriment, and elation.

Maslow felt that this aspect was very important, and he pointed out that his clinical experience indicated that psychologically healthy people quite simply *enjoyed* sexual expression more than others. Sex was a kind of game for them, where they laughed like children and played like puppies. The sex lives of these people were often characterized by great ecstasy, but they were also playful and cheerful. (His description bears repeating: "... laughter is quite as common as panting"!)[35]

Maslow's point is well taken, and the only thing I would add is this: in the loving sexual relationship, this shared cheerfulness, joy, and play become precisely a way of caring for this other person and assuming responsibility for her/him.

Psychological Intimacy

Cheerfulness, joy, and play clearly involve not only physical intimacy but psychological intimacy as well. The two persons want to know and be known by each other. Secrets are shared, and in many areas of life, something like a "code" language develops, which is understood only by the two. They develop a sense of the privacy of their lives together. As we will note below, it is not that they exclude others from their care and concern—the opposite is really the case in authentic sexual love—but rather that the two have discovered a new solitude which is not loneliness. They sense that this solitude is so good a thing that it borders on the sacred, and they respect it and value it as such. They have the freedom to welcome others into their lives, because the life which they share has a wholeness and integrity which their separate lives previously lacked.

The Unselfishness of Sexual Love

Sexual love is a feeling which changes our world and which gives directivity to our lives. It does this by creating out of two "I's" a "we," which is so intimate, so secure, and so enduring, that from now on, each can attend, imagine, think, speak, and act for the other.

When two people are in love sexually, there is a union of wants and needs and desires. Each feels the other's needs as though they were his/her own; each knows that his/her own needs are those of the other. As Fromm defines it, "Love is an active striving for the growth and happiness of the loved person."[36] Moritz Schlick, in his *Problems of Ethics,* puts the thought in a somewhat complicated way, but it is still worthy of the effort required to understand it. "The idea of a pleasant or unpleasant state of another person is, itself, a pleasant or unpleasant experience. The natural effect of these inclinations is that their bearer establishes the joyful state of others as ends of his own conduct."[37]

Maslow had commented on the same point. He noted that in a good marriage, the partners react to sickness in a characteristic way: they see it as something which happens to both of them, as a couple, and not as a misfortune of one partner alone. They act as though both were struck by the sickness, and they mobilize their forces together to meet the threat. There is total community in their suffering and total identity of their needs, because each sees the needs of the other as identical with his or her own needs.[38]

Sexual Love and the Transcendence of Self

Sexual love awakens the feeling of wanting to give and wanting to please, of wanting to give of oneself wholly and entirely, without reserve and without calculation, of wanting to share the risks, the dangers, the pain of the other person; of wanting to make sacrifices to lighten the burden of the other person. It is here that the self-transcendence of real sexual love becomes manifest and it is here that real sexual love offers a liberation from egoism which touches the whole person, because it creates a security, a joy, and a peace, without which love of the neighbor is impossible. (Sexual love is not the only way in which this security, joy, and peace can be attained. However, it is the ordinary way, and for many human beings the only way.) Sexual love gives momentum and drive and power to human existence. Only one who is accepted and affirmed by another can accept and love him/herself, and only one who can accept and affirm him/herself can accept and love others. In sexual love, each person experiences acceptance and affirmation in a way which touches every aspect and dimension of his/her being. It is an essential part of the mystery of all reality that it becomes truly itself only in going outside and beyond itself. This might be called the first law of all created being, and it is rooted in the almost incredible fact that God decided, in eternity, not to exist purely in and for himself. God is the eternal decision not to be alone, and as a result of that fact, we are here. Even purely material things exist in so far as they touch others, and they achieve their real truth when they are seen and heard, known, appreciated, and loved by us. This striving for self-transcendence is a particularly important and even essential part of our own existence, and the need, on the psychological level, for self-transcendence, is at least as great as the need for proper nourishment on the physical level. If we are deprived of this fulfillment, our suffering will be no less real than the suffering which comes from being deprived of food. There are many ways in which we seek and sometimes find self-transcendence, but one of the most profoundly satisfying is the healthy relationship which we have characterized as sexual love. We are all called to self-transcendence and we need to find a way to answer this call. For the overwhelming majority of human beings, sexual love is the way in which this vocation can and should be lived.[39]

The Creativity of Sexual Love

The creative power of sexual love springs from this new reality which has come into being, this "we" which has replaced two isolated "I's." Human beings are separated from each other; we are divided and hostile. This alienation rests on solid and factual grounds: we are, for excellent reasons, insecure, and we strive to compensate for this by manipulating and controlling others, so that we may, for a brief moment, enjoy the illusion of being secure as the result of what we have done. Whenever this isolation and mutual alienation are brought to an end, a miracle has taken place, separation has ended, and, in the words of the German poet, Rainer Maria Rilke, "two solitudes have reached out to protect, touch, and greet each other."

One of the principal reasons why love is so creative is that two people in love can see qualities and virtues in each other to which others may be oblivious. Some think, a bit cynically, that this is a case of the proverbial blindness of love. But Maslow felt that, although this may be true for people whose capacity for love is very limited, it was probably not at all true for those whom he called "self-actualizing." It seems that authentic love, far from making us blind, actually makes us more perceptive of and more alert for, those values which are more important in the other person. Psychologically healthy people are not put off by superficial blemishes or by the lack of physical perfection, as judged by contemporary standards of "beauty." They see beneath the surface, and they are attracted by character traits which are invisible to others. They are more perceptive and more intelligent in their loving, because they see others as persons and not as means to an end.[40]

Oswald Schwarz makes much the same point: "It cannot be emphasized strongly enough that this miraculous capacity which love bestows on the lovers consists in the power to discover in the object of love virtues which it *actually possesses* (the italics are mine), but which are invisible to the uninspired."[41] Earlier in the same book, Schwarz had pointed out the real reason for this: "No doubt there is a strong emotional element in it, but essentially love is a cognitive act, and indeed, it is the only way to grasp the innermost core of personality."[42] To be really known because really loved, and really loved because really known, is the ultimate human experience. It is a possibility which can be achieved in sexual love, and it is in the realization of this possibility that sexual love comes to its fulfillment. When that possibility becomes fact, then a miracle of creativity takes place.

The mysterious creativity of sexual love is rooted in the fact that all love banishes anxiety from life to a greater or lesser degree, and therefore makes it possible for those who are loved to drop their defenses, roles, and poses. This represents an immense saving in energy, making possible a concentration on *living* which is out of the question when poses must be maintained in the presence of others (and, above all, in front of oneself). In authentic sexual love, one can be, at one and the same time, psychologically naked *and* secure. (And this dropping of psychological defenses is symbolized and expressed by the physical presence of the partners to each other, unprotected and vulnerable, in the act of intercourse.)

It is precisely the creativity of sexual love which prompts Maslow to observe that, for healthy people, sex improves with familiarity and not with novelty. The conclusion would seem to be obvious: if novelty (in the sense of ever-changing partners) is needed, then there is something unhealthy and sick in one's sexual life. (Note carefully that Maslow is not counselling *routine* in sexual love; precisely as communication, sexual love will tend toward growth in knowledge, and there will be appropriate physical expression of this growth and change.)

Sexual Love and Genuine Freedom

When sexual love transforms existence by creating a "we" which is intimate, secure, and enduring, something paradoxical in the extreme happens: the self which is now *one* with the other, is more than ever concerned with the *uniqueness*, the *individuality*, and the true *freedom* of the other. There are, of course, sick relationships, where one party yields up his/her individuality to the other, but such relationships have nothing to do with love. Responsible writers on authentic sexual love stress the fact that it is characterized by concern for the individuality of the other and by the desire to foster the personal existence of the other. To love a person implies, not the possession of that person, but the affirmation of that person. Erich Fromm has some good lines on this matter, too: "Love is the foremost component of such spontaneity; not love as the dissolution of the self in another person, but love as the spontaneous affirmation of others, of the union of the individual with others on the basis of the preservation of the individual himself."[43]

This is paradoxical, because it contradicts what we would expect to be the case. If sexual love is the creation, the coming-to-be of a "we" to replace two isolated "I's," then the conclusion would seem to be that each must sacrifice his/her identity. But Maslow's comment about those whom he calls "self-actualizing" is that "they maintain a degree of individuality, of detachment, of autonomy, that seems, at first glance, to be incompatible with the kind of identification and love which I have been describing above."[44]

Authentic sexual love apparently involves and implies a kind of creative tension between individuality (being *in* and *for* oneself) and identification with the other person. This tension does not lead to the compromising of either of these attitudes or values. Properly speaking, they are never in competition, and in genuine sexual love they coexist simultaneously to a marked degree, tending to grow and increase together. Real love is not a crutch, and more than any other factor in life it promotes and fosters human existence. Authentic sexual love does not make the partners dependent on each other, at least in the ordinary sense of this word. They enjoy each other's presence on every level--spiritual, psychological, emotional, physical—and yet they know how to cope with each other's absence and can even face the death of the one they love without being shattered. Those who love this way do not lose their identity and they do not give up their individuality; in becoming one with each other, they become more distinctive as persons and stronger as individuals. Authentic sexual love seems to foster individuality without egoism, and at the same time it promotes a merging of the personalities without any loss of identity. Sexual love is a polar relationship which in some ways is analogous to a magnetic field. In a weak field, both poles are weak, but when the field is strong, so are both poles. The strength and sense of identity of each of the sexes, communally and individually, depends on the strength, the uniqueness, the individuality, the "otherness" of the opposite sex.[45]

A Brief Summary of Sexual Love

This will be a good place to summarize a number of points which have been made over the last few pages. The most important point is that sexual love is to be understood as a *unity*. It is, to be sure, a complex and multi-dimensional unity. It is not "assembled" or "put together" out of separate elements. For this reason, it is better to speak of these elements as different *dimensions*. This is a good image, because although the dimensions of an object (height, width, depth) are quite distinct and should not be confused, neither are they to be separated. In a similar way, there are many dimensions in sexual love, and a great deal of confusion is caused by using the one word "love" to refer to all of these different dimensions. For this reason, it will be helpful, in this summary, to use different words to speak of the different dimensions of sexual love.

The first dimension of sexual love is that of *libido*, the vital level on which physical union is sought. However, it is important to note that this level is not merely physiological but has important psychological components as well. It is on this level that we experience the build up of sexual energy and tension, and it is here that we experience the release of this tension in orgasm. The attempt to live on this level alone is destructive, not because there is something wrong with libido, but because libido, in order to be true to itself, needs the other dimensions of love. When libido takes its place within the multi-dimensional unity of love, then it becomes shared joy, an ecstatic moment given and received.

The second dimension of sexual love is that of *eros*. It is a dimension which is much misunderstood, and this misunderstanding has given to the adjective "erotic" some meanings which reflect the distortion of eros rather than its fulfillment. Properly understood, eros is the level of infatuation, tenderness, affection, and passion. It is the level on which the total complementarity of the sexes is felt, sensed, experienced. This level, too, if sought entirely for its own sake, is destructive, not because there is anything wrong with it, but because of the fact that, of its very own nature, it calls for fulfillment within the multi-dimensional unity of love. Within this proper framework, eros is the experience of the emotional complementarity of the sexes and is an experience of giving and receiving.

The third dimension of sexual love is *agape*—the unselfish desire of simply "being there" for the other. This is the essential human love, the love which makes us fully personal. We become genuine persons to the extent to which agape reaches into all levels of our existence. Agape is genuine love, even when it exists without the other dimensions of love which have been mentioned above, although, in the case of a man and a woman who would be suitable marriage partners, it often comes into being in connection with them. When it does, it unites and transforms them and contributes the specific "love" component to sexual love.

Note again that the task of agape is not to suppress or to negate the other dimensions of sexual love; its task is rather to unify, to integrate, and to fulfill them. Agape is the soul of sexual love, while eros and libido are its body. Libido and eros need agape in order to be fully human. When they are integrated by agape, they become ways of being there for the other on all dimensions of our being—the spiritual, the emotional, and the physical. *Agape* can be defined simply as "unselfish love," and it is this unselfish love which strives to transform us precisely as sexed and sexual beings, by finding in eros and libido various ways of "being there" for the other unselfishly. Sexual love, as we have defined it, is this fully human love, a synthesis of agape, eros, and libido. In this synthesis, these three loves do not compete for our attention, nor do they ask us to balance their claims in some precarious manner. It is agape which redirects our sexuality itself, and all forms of sexual expression in which we engage; and when we seek the good of the other, and do this precisely as sexual beings, then our sexuality fulfills the purposes which are immanent to it, and we become the persons that God calls us to be.

5.

Problems in Reaching Psycho-Sexual Maturity

We have often noted that the central task which our sexuality imposes on us is that of integration. In terms of the three dimensions of sexual love, this insight can now be expressed as follows: the human task is that of insuring that our entire sexual existence, and specifically the spheres of libido and eros, are given shape and form by agape and are a revelation of agape. This comes about when we act in such a way as to make libido and eros share in the other-directedness of agape, so that they come to manifest the great human mystery: the mystery that we are truly ourselves only in *giving,* only in finding the center of our being in another, and that it is precisely such giving which confers human fulfillment on us. It is only in losing ourselves that we find ourselves.

There are a number of problems which arise in connection with the progress of the individual toward psycho-sexual maturity and in connection with the development of attitudes toward sexuality in society at large, and all of these problems should be examined from the standpoint of the mystery of sexual love and its essential other-directedness. Problems in sexual development, as well as the failure to reach sexual maturity, should be seen, not as the violation of law or taboo, but rather as forms of conduct which conspire against the essential other-directedness of healthy human sexuality. If our choices in these matters are sinful (and they can be), this is the case because these choices represent the failure to integrate libido and eros with agape; that is, they fail to integrate love and sexual expression.

Autoerotic Behavior

The first form of inadequate sexual integration (and usually the first in time as well) is masturbation (achieving sexual release by oneself through stimulating the erogenous zones of the body). This seems to occur for longer or shorter periods of time during adolescence in almost a hundred per cent of the male population, and it occurs often enough in later life as well. (It seems to be somewhat less prevalent among girls and women, for reasons which we will comment on later.) Masturbation is a symptom of a sexuality which is striving to make itself independent on the level of libido, and which is either not yet aware of or rejects the essential other-directedness of human sexuality. It is worth examining, not in order to stigmatize such conduct as "sinful," but rather, so that we can see it in terms of the difficulties which we all have in attaining psychological sexual maturity. Practically speaking, it seems almost inevitable that masturbation will be practiced sometime during the sexual development of the human male, and this inevitability suggests that the self-righteous horror with which the practice was often viewed in the past is completely out of place. Just as out of place are the deep and destructive guilt feelings of those who have practiced masturbation. At the same time, masturbation should be seen as a troubling sign of just how unintegrated our sexuality is, and of how difficult the achievement of sexual maturity is for all of us. The practice is an infantile fixation which *can* be a sign of arrested sexual development. It should not be stamped as "perversion," but neither is it a particularly healthy use of our sexual powers. Infantile fixations such as masturbation can, if engaged in habitually, hamper the development of psychosexual maturity. Avoiding such practices involves a good deal of self-control, but such self-control is not to be sought for its own sake but precisely for the contribution which it can make to mature sexual love. Self-control which is exercised for such a reason is a very good thing, and it is here that frank and honest sex education by parents can do a world of good by presenting such self-control as a real value. In this matter, as in all others which touch our sexuality, authentic sexual love is the norm and criterion according to which certain practices can be judged as unworthy of our free choice.

Failures in the Realm of Eros

Failures in this area have given the Greek word *eros* some unfortunate connotations. Properly understood, eros is the sphere in which we experience, feel, and enjoy fulfillment in the other person, who is, in every respect, complementary to us. It should be a *mutual* experience, in which the two, who are now one, experience the total complementarity of their sexual selves. This experience gives us a sense of joy, contentment, and well-being which suffuses every level of personal existence—the spiritual, the emotional, and the physical. Failure occurs when this experience is not that of the *two* (that "we" which is the intimate and secure "new being" which comes into existence in sexual love), but rather only that of an "I" which sees eros uniquely in terms of self-fulfillment. This leads to the effort to possess that sense of well-being for oneself, and it makes one's own emotional experience, one's own sensuality, an end or goal of action. What results is a parody of self-fulfillment and a type of pleasure which is not fully human. Failures in this area appear in a number of characteristic ways, some of which have important legal and social dimensions that raise questions of law and of public policy.

One manifestation of the failure to achieve sexual integration in this area might be called the "gourmet" approach: it is the view which sees sexual behavior primarily as the source of emotional satisfaction and pleasure for oneself, and sees the other as a means to this end. For the sexual gourmet, pleasure is not the result or the accompaniment of a truly creative act, but is rather sought for itself. Here Paul Tillich's remark is very much to the point: "The pain/pleasure principle is valid only in sick, uncentered and therefore uncreative, unfree life."[46] (Note once again that Tillich is not suspicious of pleasure—either sexual pleasure or any other kind. He is simply pointing out, correctly, that genuinely human pleasure is always the *concomitant* of a creative human act.)

A common variety of the sexual gourmet is the "erotic engineer," who places all the emphasis on technique, in order to extract the last ounce of pleasure from sexual activity. The problem with this is that technique is useful for the manipulation of *things*, but it is depersonalizing if applied to human beings. Again, we have to be extremely careful in talking about this problem because it should never be suggested that intense sexual pleasure is for some reason suspect. The key word in the definition of the erotic engineer is "extract," which connotes concentration on oneself and which makes pleasure itself the *goal* of action. The gourmet and the erotic engineer are never satisfied, and sexual experience offers them no real fulfillment. Rather, it becomes an obsession which leads to ever more exotic and bizarre ways of getting pleasure.[47]

In the life of the erotic engineer, sexual behavior is divorced from personal commitment, and when this happens, some very dangerous disorientations put in an appearance. The personality itself begins to disintegrate, and a symptom of this is the growing confusion between the domination/submission rituals (which originated as a successful adaptation to the needs of animals living in communal groups), and sexual conduct in the proper sense of the word. Masochism and sadism (the deriving of sexual "pleasure" from inflicting pain on oneself or on others, respectively) appear, but such "pleasure" is only a sick and obsessive parody and has nothing to do with the shared joy of fulfillment which is of the essence of a truly human sensuality.

It is important to emphasize once more that the approach of the sexual gourmet and the erotic engineer is a failure in sexual integration, not because it is "too sexual." These approaches fail because they are not truly sexual at all. They are not the response of *this woman* to *this man, this man to this woman,* because both the gourmet and the erotic engineer are totally indifferent to the personal existence of the one with whom they engage in sexual activity. Failure to integrate the erotic dimension into a truly human sexuality is destructive, not because it is too animalistic or because it leads to intense pleasure. We belong to the animal kingdom and sensuality is a gift of God. But sensuality needs agape, that personal love which alone can make it fully human. Pleasure will be a human experience and incomparably more intense and fulfilling only when it is not sought for itself.

Another form taken by the failure to integrate eros in love could be called "sex as a spectator sport," and it includes all of the "needs" satisfied by the pornography industry. This approach also aims at securing pleasure for the individual, and it offers this pleasure by giving the individual something to look or to gaze at. But in doing this, it strips sex of its communicative character, and sees it only as a private response to visual stimuli. And without communication, sex cannot be a personal act and pleasure cannot be a component of a personal response. The voyeur (one who finds pleasure only in looking) is a sexual failure, and sex as a spectator sport is a sign of the absence of authentically sexual love. If engaged in for protracted periods, it may make sexual love difficult if not impossible. Such forms of behavior are a rejection of the values inherent in human sexuality, and this is the precise reason for criticizing them.

Pornography as a Social Problem

Although voyeurism is a perversion, pornography is an industry, and there are some social and legal aspects of the question which should be mentioned here, even though they do not belong to the question of sexual morality properly speaking. It is not really correct to call pornography (or, more accurately, the dissemination of pornographic materials) a victimless crime. Sexual perversion is not an entirely private matter. We are all affected by what we see and what we read, and then we proceed to affect others as a result of it. Education is built on the principle that exposure to intellectually and esthetically sound material will foster the development of the human person. The obvious correlative to this is that exposure to distorted and warped material interferes with the development of the person and is likely to produce a warped and distorted human being.

Unfortunately, pornography is often opposed for the wrong reasons. In the proper sense of the word, the sexualization of life is a very good thing, and anything which impedes the authentic sexualization of life should be opposed. This underlines the real problem with pornography: it works *against* the healthy sexualization of life, and this is the only valid and safe reason for opposing it. Many people (and very many who think of themselves as religious) are embarrassed by their sexuality. They object to any treatment of sexual themes in the arts and view these themes as pornographic. This position is absurd, because life is essentially sexual, and art cannot dispense with the depiction of life. But it is worse than absurd, because when pornography is not properly defined or when it is opposed for the wrong reasons, it becomes increasingly difficult to oppose it for the right reasons. Opposition to pornography which is based on a deep esteem for and appreciation of human sexuality is safe; opposition on any other grounds is not.

Is some form of censorship the answer to the pornography problem? In general it is not, because censorship is usually not an apt, appropriate, and effective means of dealing with it. We are rightly suspicious when government meddles in our private lives, and we certainly have no need of committees of officious bureaucrats to decide what we may read and what we may not. Furthermore, censorship always gives the porn peddler the opportunity to pose as a first amendment hero and a leader in the defense of free speech. However, some *regulation* of pornography seems appropriate. (Censorship implies that permission must be given and approval secured *before* material is printed or copied; regulation implies that the law may determine the places where pornographic materials may be sold, the age of those to whom they may be offered, etc.) Regulation is appropriate because people do have the right to protect their neighborhoods from what offends and disgusts them. Furthermore, the majority in a given social or political group has the right to have its standards respected, provided the real rights of others are not infringed on.

However, regulation is only a short term, *ad hoc* solution. The only effective long-term answer to the problem is an ethos (a system of human values) which sees the healthy sexualization of life as an ideal, and which has learned to express and embody this ideal in all of the arts—in music, sculpture, painting, dance, in the novel, in poetry, in drama, and in film. An essential task of art is to promote the healthy sexualization of life, and a society which is successful in this respect will have no really serious pornography problem. Healthy sexuality is incomparably more intriguing and infinitely more fulfilling than sick sexuality. The only answer to pornography is a high esteem of sexual love and the willingness to accept it as the great gift which it is. This is why it is very important to identify and reject prudish and puritanical attitudes toward sex; pornography should not be met with righteous wrath but with disgust. But note carefully that the rejection of such prudish and puritanical attitudes about sex does not mean that sexual behavior should "go public" or that it is a good thing to babble incessantly about sex. There is a privacy which is proper to sexual love, although the specific form taken by such privacy is conditioned by cultural factors.

One final point is important. Pornography involves elements other than the overtly sexual. Pornography is closely related to the approach of the sexual gourmet and the erotic engineer and therefore it often contains strong elements of sadism and masochism. Some forms of violence, both in spectator sports and on film, should probably be judged in this light. Much of the "sex" on TV, to which many groups object today, is not pornographic in any serious way, although it is often quite silly and poses a threat to authentic sexuality for precisely that reason. In fact, most of the "sex" on TV really seems designed to titillate excessively naive adolescents, and the real problem with the so-called suggestive lines and themes of contemporary mass entertainment is that they trivialize or banalize human sexuality and are therefore not authentically sexual. Sexuality is a splendid thing and deserves better treatment.

Homosexuality

Homosexuality is discussed at this point in the book because it is best understood as a symptom of psycho-sexual development which has been blocked or has "stalled" at a stage short of maturity. The problem of the moral evaluation of homosexuality, and of homosexual behavior is difficult enough in itself, and it is further complicated by the question of legal and social discrimination against homosexuals. These questions are much discussed today, and very different answers are given—answers which are a microcosm of the views of our contemporaries on the nature of human sexuality and on the possibility of making objective judgments about ways of acting which are not in accord with the purpose of human life. For this reason, the topic will be treated here more thoroughly than the problem and the frequency of homosexuality itself would seem to demand.

Sin, Sickness, or Alternate Life-Style?

Is homosexuality a sin? There has been a strong tendency in the Christian tradition to regard homosexual *acts* as sinful (i.e. as "bad," morally wrong). There were various reasons for this, but the most important were the texts from both the Old Testament and the New Testament which condemn homosexual activity in very harsh terms. For example, traditional Jewish and Christian interpretations viewed the destruction of the cities of Sodom and Gomorrah as God's punishment for the sins of homosexuality which the inhabitants were committing.[48] In the New Testament, the text of Romans 1:26 played a key role in Christian attitudes toward homosexual activity, because it is there that Paul speaks of homosexual acts as the ultimate sign and symptom of man's perversion and alienation from God.[49] In recent years there have been some attempts in Catholic circles (and even more in some liberal Protestant churches) to mitigate the harshness of these older views, on the grounds that the Bible gives us, in this matter, not a divinely authorized judgment on homosexual activity, but rather a record of historically and culturally determined attitudes of Jews and early Christians. But these attempts have been rather partisan in tone and have not been accepted by biblical scholars.

Apart from the question of interpreting the scriptural texts, there are other factors today which have led some to call for a re-evaluation of Christian attitudes toward the homosexual. We are more aware today of the power of psychological compulsions and therefore of the fact that some of our acts are not as free as they might seem.[50]

Since 1970, Catholic authorities have felt obliged, on several different occasions, to reject these liberalizing tendencies. In October 1986, Cardinal Joseph Ratzinger, Prefect of the Congregation for the Faith, in a letter addressed to Catholic bishops throughout the world, reaffirmed the traditional Catholic position with great clarity in these words: "Although the particular inclination of the homosexual person is not a sin, it is a more or less strong tendency ordered toward an intrinsic moral evil; and thus, the inclination itself must be seen as an objective disorder." In the same document, Ratzinger outlined church teaching on the immorality of homosexual behavior, and described as "erroneous" the claim that scripture is silent on the subject or is no longer applicable to contemporary life.[51]

Is homosexuality a sickness? For years, this description was able to secure a measure of tolerance and sympathy for homosexuals, but today homosexual activists object very strongly to this designation. The American Psychiatric Association changed its nomenclature in 1973 and began referring to homosexuality as a "disturbance" rather than as a neurosis or a form of neurotic behavior. However, it seems clear that there were factors other than medical which played a role in the various changes in nomenclature which the APsA has issued in the past decade. (And it is worth noting that when the APsA changed its classification of homosexuality from "mental disorder" to "sexual orientation disturbance," the Board of Trustees specifically refused to refer to homosexual orientation as "normal.")[52] In fact, a majority of psychiatrists today seem to agree that homosexual behavior is a symptom of psychological development which has been arrested at some stage short of maturity, and many psychiatrists mention that in their clinical practice, homosexual behavior is frequently associated with severe emotional illness.[53]

Is homosexuality simply an "alternate life style," a different way of expressing one's sexuality, and as such is it to be valued no differently from heterosexuality? This is the position of almost all homosexual activists and apologists today. John McNeill, a Catholic priest, tried in his book, *The Church and the Homosexual*, to argue historically and theologically for this position, but after the book had been on sale for a year, church authorities ordered it withdrawn, and McNeill himself was told to keep quiet on the question. (McNeill maintained this silence until the fall of 1986, when his refusal to obey his superiors on this question brought the issue to a head and led to his departure from his religious order. His position, strongly rejected by most Catholics and conservative Protestants, has won some adherents in some of the more liberal Protestant denominations.)[54]

Some Definitions

The word "homosexuality" is used in two senses and it is very important to distinguish them. First, it can refer to an attitude or *orientation* (a kind of inclination of one's character or nature), and second, it can refer to an *action* or class of actions, or to the *willingness* to engage in such actions. One may have a homosexual orientation without ever engaging in homosexual acts and without ever being willing to engage in such acts. Although popular usage varies, for clarity and accuracy, I would suggest that the word "homosexuality" be used only to refer to the *orientation*, and that is the sense in which it will be used here.

Homosexuality as an orientation could be defined in this way: it is a *preference*, on the part of *adults*, for *sexual behavior* with members of their own sex. The italicized words here are very important. The word *preference* assumes that opportunities for healthy contact with members of the opposite sex are present. Such opportunities may be lacking, for example, in prisons, in some boarding schools, and in similar situations.

What occurs under such abnormal circumstances is not, properly speaking, homosexuality, because there is no real preference being exercised. (This, of course, is not to assert that such apparently homosexual conduct is acceptable or tolerable. It is harmful in a variety of ways, but it should not be confused with homosexuality in the proper sense.)

Furthermore, homosexuality is an *adult* phenomenon. The word should not be used to refer to certain kinds of sexual fixation or conduct which may take place during adolescence. At the beginning of adolescence no one has achieved a mature heterosexual adaptation, and some of the ways of expressing affection which children learn in the family may easily be applied to those who are esteemed and admired. Ordinarily such conduct is not homosexual (by definition), but there can be some danger in these situations, and the older "role models" should be aware of this. Note also that some forms of what appears to be group homosexual conduct among adolescent males are not really homosexual in the proper sense of the word, but are probably best interpreted as experiments in "trying out one's sexual equipment." Such behavior is hardly helpful in achieving sexual maturity, and it may even do considerable harm, but it belongs properly under the heading of masturbation and not homosexuality.[55]

The third element of the definition of homosexuality is extremely important. Homosexuality involves a preference for *sexual behavior* with those of the same sex. This phrase means "actions which lead to physical fulfillment or orgasm" or "infatuation which moves toward physical, genital fulfillment." It is *extremely important not to confuse close friendships between men or between women with homosexuality*, because such non-homosexual friendships constitute a very high human value.[56] What marks them as genuine is the absence of specifically sensual or erotic components, but it should be noted that although the elements of physical sexuality are absent, various signs of friendship are appropriate. These signs vary with the time and the culture; if any doubts arise as to their appropriateness, a practical guide would be to ask what signs of friendship and affection are appropriate between brothers or between sisters within the same family.

How Frequent Is Homosexuality?

There seems to be some exaggeration here by homosexuals and this probably reflects an understandable concern to make homosexuality acceptable; modern society has an odd tendency to settle moral questions by taking a poll, and concluding that whatever is widespread must be morally acceptable. The best studies indicate that in Europe and the Americas the homosexual proportion of the male population runs from three to five percent, and for women the figure runs from one to two percent. A generation ago, the Kinsey Report asserted that four percent of American males were exclusively homosexual; it is highly unlikely that the figure has changed.[57]

In regard to the past, it is often asserted that Ancient Greece, at least from the late fifth century on, was a homosexual civilization, in the sense that homosexual activity was accepted as normal, or even idealized, but this is not accurate. What does seem to have been accepted among the leisured classes during a certain period (after 400 B.C.; there is no trace of it in Homeric times) was not precisely sexual behavior between mature men, but rather *sexual behavior of men with boys*. The rise of this peculiar kind of homosexuality seems to coincide with the decline in the position of women—in Athenian society, for example, they were not deemed worthy of education and were secluded.[58]

Making a Judgment about Homosexuality

What kind of judgment should we make about homosexuality and homosexual conduct? The implication of this question is that we ought to be judgmental about homosexuality, just as we ought to be about all aspects of sexual conduct. To be judgmental means to strive to make solid judgments, based on evidence, about whether a given form of conduct leads to psycho-sexual maturity and therefore whether, in the deepest sense of the word, it is *good* for the human being. The refusal to make such judgments is not motivated by kindness, or tolerance, or respect for human freedom; it is motivated by contempt for ourselves and for our fellow human beings.

The basis for making a judgment about homosexuality is the insight that sexual love is properly the love of man for woman, woman for man; only in such a love are *all* aspects of personal complementarity brought into play—the spiritual, the emotional, and the physical. To be a fully mature person is to be essentially oriented toward *the other kind of person*. Sexuality is not a merely physical characteristic; it touches all levels and dimensions of the human person. This means that sexual love in the proper sense must respect the psychological and physical structures which characterize us as intelligent animals. This implies that homosexual activity cannot be the full expression of sexual love, in the proper sense of this term.

The Causes of Homosexuality

This question is much discussed (and often hotly debated) today. The homosexual orientation is complex, and there seem to be many factors which play a causative role: genetic and biological, cultural, psychological. It may be that in many cases of homosexuality all of these factors are involved, or it might be more accurate to speak of several quite different forms which the homosexual orientation can take, and to distinguish them by the roles which these different factors play. Forms of overt behavior which seem quite similar to all but the trained psychiatrist may have quite different roots and may call for very different treatment.

The last word on the question has obviously not been spoken, although it seems clear that, even if we admit the possibility of various causes, psychological factors predominate. This is the view of a large majority of those psychiatrists who have addressed the question and they have amassed impressive evidence in support of their position.

The French priest and psychiatrist, Ignace Lepp, summarized a broad consensus, when he concluded that the homosexual orientation is the result of an early fixation on one parent, which has inhibited normal sexual development.[59] The classical statement of the nature of this fixation was made by Irving Bieber, in a paper which he gave before the Society of Medical Psychiatrists in New York, and which was later published under the title *Homosexuality: A Psychiatric Study of Male Homosexuals* (New York, 1962).

Bieber summarized his own experience in treating homosexuals, as well as the clinical experience of seventy-seven affiliated psychoanalysts in the following way: the family pattern was usually disturbed. The mother tended to be overprotective and emotionally (and at times physically) seductive. The father was often detached, remote, and sometimes overtly hostile. Bieber concluded that, in order to promote the healthy sexual development of the boy, the father is extremely important: "A constructive, supportive, warmly related father precludes the possibility of a homosexual son."[60]

Saghir and Robbins, writing eleven years after Bieber's results were published, provide interesting statistical confirmation of Bieber's argument. Eighty-four percent of the homosexuals they interviewed reported that their fathers were often emotionally absent, despite their physical presence at home, while only eighteen percent of the heterosexual control group made the same point.[61]

Many psychiatrists speak of the homosexual orientation as a form of inadequate ego-development,[62] characterized by a lack of sexual identity, which results in the inability to cope with the challenge of mature sexuality. In the view of these psychiatrists, the homosexual is afraid of mature heterosexual union because he lacks a sense of identity and worth. This insecurity prompts the fear that if he gives himself to the other (that is, to the *truly other*, who is in every respect the counterpart of what he is as a male person), then he will lose himself irreparably; in other words, the homosexual looks for a form of sexual release which does not make the demands on his self-confidence and his identity which true heterosexual love does.[63] One indication of this is that studies of male homosexuals have indicated that their encounters are brief, often anonymous, but numerous.[64]

We can conclude these comments with another point made by Ignace Lepp.[65] Male homosexuality seems to be the result of a definite pattern of child-rearing and acculturation—a pattern which does not seem to be a healthy or desirable one—and it seems clear that it would be worth taking all appropriate steps to prevent a child from receiving this type of conditioning. The form which these steps should take is that of creating and fostering a healthy climate within the family, which promotes identification with the parent of the same sex and at the same time promotes the creative encounter with the parent of the opposite sex. In the long run, the healthy sexual love of the parents for each other will be the most helpful factor in creating such a climate.

The causes of female homosexuality are much more obscure.[66] The number of female homosexuals is far less than that of their male counterparts, and female homosexuality seems to be less often associated with other forms of psychopathology. A common element in the background of most female homosexuals who have been studied seems to be a strong anti-heterosexual pattern in the home (although this sounds suspiciously like rephrasing the problem rather than finding a solution). As a result of this pattern, relationships with boys are discouraged, while "crushes" on girls are either disregarded or even secretly encouraged. The rise of the women's liberation movement has, at times and for various complex reasons, actually promoted lesbianism as the ideal form of love for women who wish to escape fully from masculine domination.[67]

The Moral Assessment of Homosexuality

People sometimes ask if homosexuality is sinful, morally wrong. Since we have argued that, in the proper sense, homosexuality refers to an *orientation* and not to an action or a decision, it seems clear that words such as "sinful" or "morally wrong" make no sense when applied to homosexuality as such. Only decisions and choices can be morally good or morally bad, and the homosexual orientation as such is not ordinarily the object of either a decision or a choice.

However, we have also pointed out that, whether it is described as a form of neurosis or as a "sexual orientation disturbance," homosexuality is not an ideal way of using one's sexual faculties, and is often the result of a family situation which can only be called unhealthy. This means that, although the orientation in itself is not the object of choice, when one becomes aware of such an orientation and then pursues a course of action which makes it increasingly difficult to correct, then the orientation is ratified and becomes the object of a decision. At this point, under certain circumstances, such a decision could be morally wrong or sinful.[68] This is probably what Cardinal Ratzinger meant in his November 1986 letter to the Catholic Bishops. The terminology which he uses is not entirely felicitous (particularly in translation), but he is probably referring to precisely such a situation when he makes this point: "When people engage in homosexual activity, they confirm within themselves a disordered sexual inclination which is essentially self-indulgent."

Often the word "homosexuality" is used (somewhat inaccurately, I believe) to refer not to the orientation but to homosexual acts or homosexual behavior, and here the moral evaluation is more difficult. It is possible that such acts may result from the willingness to accept the unhealthy form of psycho-sexual development which homosexuality represents, and from the deliberate rejection of the truly human encounter with the opposite sex. Some moral theologians have tried to deal with this problem by referring to homosexual acts as "ontically evil," but because the word "evil" is so closely associated with morally bad *decisions*, it would be better to use the terminology suggested by others in the field. Richard McCormick, for example, refers to such acts as "not normative";[69] Eugene Kennedy calls them "not human expression at full term";[70] and Charles Curran affirms that these acts "can never become an ideal."[71]

It is important to remember that our external actions cannot, *in themselves,* be morally good or morally bad; only the conscious choice of actions which are "not normative" or "never an ideal" or "in themselves unworthy of being chosen" can be morally bad, or sinful. Our responsibility depends on the degree of knowledge and freedom we have in making such apparent choices, and since the homosexual orientation itself frequently results from an unhealthy family situation which was not created by the homosexual himself, it is possible that much homosexual activity is not the object of genuinely free choice, and therefore should not be called "sinful" in any sense. Certainly in the case of one who is making a serious attempt to combat homosexual practice, an occasional lapse should be no reason for obsessive feelings of guilt, and such persons should be confident that the direction which they have given their lives is good.

On the other hand, if homosexual acts result from the general willingness to engage in such activity, which objectively falls so far short of the human ideal, then it would seem hard to avoid some degree of moral responsibility. But here, as in all moral questions, the degree of responsibility depends on the knowledge which the individual has of the harmfulness of homosexual activity and on the freedom of the individual in respect to the choice of such acts.

Attitudes toward Homosexuals

Some of the mockery and most of the violence directed at homosexuals are probably an expression of repressed homosexual tendencies in the overtly heterosexual population. Such tendencies are present in the healthy human psyche, and their presence is no cause for alarm. However, fear of these tendencies can sometimes cause us to act in a cruel and inhuman way. Such conduct is never justifiable and contemptuous references to homosexuals should be kept out of the public forum. However, when homosexual activists insist that *any* criticism of homosexual activity as a deviation or a less-than-perfect fulfillment of our sexual potential constitutes "psychological violence," this should be stamped as trendy and irresponsible nonsense. Homosexual conduct and behavior do not constitute an equally valid, alternate "life-style," and any implication that they do should be rejected. To insist on this point is not to show contempt for homosexuals; rather, the opposite is the case. Homosexuality is a disturbance of the emotional life which can, under some circumstances, be treated. Those suffering from such disturbances should be helped to find such treatment, so that they stand a chance for a more normal and fulfilling life. To effectively deny them such treatment, on the grounds that homosexuality is not a pathology but simply an alternate form of sexual expression, is not only insensitive; it is cruel.[72]

Homosexuality, Discrimination, and the Law

The question of the relation of homosexuals to the law is complex and involves two distinct issues: the first is that of the decriminalization of most forms of homosexual activity and the second is that of banning discrimination against homosexuals in employment, housing, the military, and other areas of life.

In regard to decriminalizing homosexual activity, it seems clear that laws which attempt to regulate the private sexual conduct of consenting adults simply do not work because they are, practically speaking, unenforceable. Laws which cannot work are bad laws and they should be repealed. The repeal of such laws does not imply that the previously banned conduct is now to be deemed acceptable or good; repeal simply means that the legislative body now sees that the regulation of such conduct is not the appropriate concern of civil law. Civil law does not and should not deal, for example, with alcoholism or excessive drinking as long as this is simply a private failing and has no effect on the rights of others, but this hardly implies that alcoholism is desirable, either for the individual or for society. Suicide is not a desirable form of conduct, but it would be rather silly to make attempted suicide a crime (perhaps some would suggest a capital offense?).

The question of discrimination against homosexuals is more complex. It is manifestly unjust to discriminate against those who have a homosexual *orientation,* but it would seem that when homosexuality is *only* an orientation, it is usually not the object of discrimination, because others will not be aware of it.

However, because the homosexual orientation itself is a relatively severe psychological and emotional disturbance, those who have this orientation could well be counselled to avoid certain kinds of work which might lead to homosexual behavior or tempt them strongly in this direction. A homosexual in the wrong line of work may well be led to engage in homosexual activity which will make treatment of his own problems more difficult and which, more importantly, may do immense harm to others, particularly young people. In general, all jobs or tasks which would bring the homosexual into contact with others of the same sex (particularly younger people) in non-public situations should be avoided (for example, scoutmasters, teachers in boarding schools, and similar positions).

More generally when homosexuality is not simply an orientation but implies a general willingness to engage in homosexual acts and especially the demand that such conduct be accepted and approved by society at large, then society has a right to reject this demand. Society should never allow itself to be told that such disturbances of the emotional life and of sexual orientation are normal, and that the conduct which manifests such disturbances is acceptable; and just as we should never accept the premise that even the milder forms of mental illness are not really illnesses at all but simply alternate forms of mental health, in the same way society and its members have the right to view homosexuality as a disturbance of the ego functions and to refuse to regard its manifestations as normal or acceptable.[73]

Just as the prevention of homosexual acts between consenting adults should be outside the province of civil law, so, for other reasons, the prevention of discrimination against homosexuals is not the business of the law. This is the case, because discrimination is directed, as a matter of fact, not against those who merely have a homosexual orientation, but against those who demand acceptance of homosexual behavior as an alternate "life style." As a practical matter, the best approach is to simply have the law ignore the question of homosexuality and not deal with it either negatively or positively. This is particularly important in this country because of the unfortunate perception that any form of conduct which is in any way protected by law is morally acceptable.

There are good reasons for combatting the notion that homosexuality is simply an alternate life style. Presumably all are aware that homosexuality is not contagious in the same way as the flu, and it is clear that mere association with homosexuals will not do any harm to adult heterosexuals. It also seems evident that when young people come from a healthy family situation, the mere presence of homosexual teachers in a school will not threaten their attainment of normal sexual identity and of a healthy heterosexual orientation (assuming, of course, that they are not the victims of homosexual molestation). However, many family situations are not healthy and many more are marginal. Boys coming from such disturbed family situations may have considerable difficulty in achieving sexual identity. They may tend, amid all of the other confusions of adolescence, to flee from the challenging encounter with the opposite sex, and if they are told by people whom they admire that such immature conduct is quite acceptable, they may believe it and never attain psycho-sexual maturity. There are many difficulties for the adolescent male en route to achieving sexual identity, and he can be greatly helped if he lives in a climate of opinion which rejects homosexuality as an acceptable life style, rather than in one which accepts it.[74]

This is not only true on an individual basis; it is also true when homosexual conduct becomes accepted in a society. When it is accepted, the capacity of many members of the society to achieve sexual integration will be limited. In this sense, homosexuality *can* spread. Emotional disturbances are rarely a private matter, and when unhealthy responses to life's challenges are accepted as normal, the capacity of many persons to make a healthy response will be correspondingly diminished.

The Question of Homosexuality in Religious Life and in the Priesthood

The question of homosexuals in religious life (that is, in religious orders or congregations, as these are found in the Catholic church and in some Protestant churches) has been much discussed in recent years. It seems clear that actual homosexual conduct is simply contrary to the vow of chastity and that one who engages in such activity should be separated from the religious community or order. This is even more the case when the individual, as not infrequently happens, flaunts his or her homosexual conduct in front of religious superiors, in order to provoke them or to make a statement or to launch a crusade for "homosexual rights" and the like. In such cases, superiors should act swiftly and firmly. If they do not, the harm to the order and the church can be enormous.

The question of admitting to religious life candidates who have a homosexual orientation is different and more complex, but the following points can be helpful in making a judgment. An isolated homosexual experience in early adolescence, particularly if only with one partner, and not continued, is insignificant (and, as noted above, probably is not properly referred to as homosexuality). However, if homosexual activity is continued into late adolescence, this is not a good sign, and it may indicate that such activity is becoming habitual. Moreover, such conduct can well be a symptom of some serious psychological problems. This is particularly the case if the homosexual activity has occurred with any frequency or with more than one partner; such persons should not be received into the religious order without careful psychological testing, and without professional evaluation of the applicant's capacity and commitment to lead a celibate life.

Everything which is said here about entry into religious life should also be applied to life in a seminary where students study for the priesthood and to the life of the celibate priest as well. It is of the nature of religious life and (to a slightly lesser degree) of the life of the celibate clergy to bring members of the same sex into close contact. For the heterosexual individual this poses no problem, but for the homosexual the danger of moving from homosexual orientation to homosexual activity will be very great, and this can cause immense harm to the religious order and to the church. Religious superiors, rectors of seminaries, and spiritual directors have very serious obligations to the church, the Christian community, in this matter. It may be that the present shortage of vocations is tempting some of these superiors to allow persons to remain in religious life and in the seminary who do not belong there and who are already causing much scandal and will cause much more in coming years.[75]

Some Conclusions

Authentic sexual love is essentially heterosexual, because it is only in such love that the complementarity of the sexes on all levels of human existence—physical, psychological, and spiritual—is respected. This love is of very great value for individuals, for families, and for society as a whole. Everything should be done to present heterosexual love as an ideal, and everything should be done to prevent the acceptance of homosexual activity as an equally valid, alternate way of living out one's sexuality. Those with homosexual orientations should be treated with sympathy, and if they are desirous of normalizing their affective preferences, they should be given the opportunity. The situation is not nearly as hopeless as it was thought to be.

If those with homosexual orientations engage in homosexual activity, they may very often be excused of grave subjective guilt on the grounds that they are suffering from a serious emotional disturbance which limits their freedom in respect to certain choices. But a homosexual orientation is unfortunate, and homosexual activity is a way of acting which falls far short of the human ideal. Everything should be done to help the homosexual who realizes this to find a place in the church and in the larger society where (s)he will be able to attain inner peace. Everything should be done to combat the destructive propaganda of those who refuse to face this fact.

6.

Marriage and Sexual Love

We have repeatedly emphasized that the term "sexual love" is not a synonym for sexual intercourse. Sexual love is a way of being in love, a way of *being there* for the other, and sexual intercourse is, ideally, a particularly important way of expressing this. Marriage, on the other hand, is an institution—a structure or pattern of activity within a society which is designed to secure some good for the society at large and for the groups and individuals who are more immediately affected.

Marriage: Its Forms and Purposes

The institution of marriage has taken many forms in the course of history, and these forms reflect different conceptions of the roles of men and women and differing views of what the real values of life are. In class societies, the continuation of the family line may be all important, at least for the upper classes, and in such societies, some form of the arranged marriage is often the norm. In more loosely structured or mobile societies, romantic marriage may be the ideal. Sometimes marriage is seen as the institution which provides children, who are necessary for the economic well-being of the family, while at other times, children are wanted simply to be loved and nurtured. More prosaically, marriage may provide security for women and instant sex for men (although this is less and less the case today).

These various goals and purposes do not have any inherent connection with sexual love as we have defined it, but the fact that most of them have become less appealing and less accepted today has had a destabilizing effect on the institution of marriage. Perhaps this is not entirely a bad thing. It might be acceptable for marriage to serve, incidentally, some of the purposes mentioned, but I believe that the value of marriage as an institution should be judged by its effectiveness in serving, fostering, and promoting sexual love, as we have defined that term, and not by its usefulness in achieving any of the goals mentioned above.[76]

The institution of marriage in our own society is quite malleable; it is in many respects undetermined and it is ready to take on the shape and form which we give it. There are a large number of ways in which marriage can be lived; it is really up to the couple to decide what they want to make of it, and in this matter there are fewer conventions today than in the past. This means that today the couple is free to play a larger role in determining the concrete form taken by their marriage; but as always when we are given greater freedom, we are given greater responsibility. Conventions can be stifling or stabilizing (and usually they are both), but when they come to play a less important role in shaping marriages, then married people themselves have to become much more attentive to the various factors which can make for success or failure in marriage and they have to ask how each of them may foster or threaten sexual love. This is the genuine *asceticism* of marriage, which touches the whole life of the couple—work and play, friendships, families, property, possessions, and all other earthly values besides. Each partner in marriage must always face this question: Will I put each of these values (and all of them together) in second place (or somewhere farther down the list) for the love of this woman, the love of this man? If I cannot, then I should not marry.[77]

People sometimes ask today if marriage has a future. If this is the same as asking whether marriage and the nuclear family should continue to be regarded as an ideal or whether they should be replaced by some form of communal living or sequential polygamy, then I believe that the answer is an unqualified "yes" to marriage. Marriage in this sense, in which permanence and exclusivity are at least recognized as an ideal, is indispensable for *human* life. There is a vacuum in the human heart which can be filled in only two ways. For those who have the special calling, it can be filled by the all-encompassing relationship with God which can properly be called "being in love with God." This call finds expression in the religious orders, as they exist in the Catholic church and in some Protestant churches (and is evidently experienced by some men and women who are not called to life in such a community, but who continue to live in the everyday world). For those who do not have this special calling, it can be filled only when a man and woman find the meaning and purpose of their existence in loving each other. It is this need and the possibility of satisfying it on which the demand for permanence and exclusivity in marriage is based.

At the same time, it seems obvious that many of the concrete details which characterize the institution of marriage at any particular historical moment both can and should change. Some of these concrete details may well have no future and may deserve none.

The Essence of Marriage

Ideally, marriage is a uniquely viable way of fostering sexual love. It could be defined in this way: it is a commitment of man and woman to each other in which they state publicly, in the presence of God and their fellow human beings, their intention to love each other all of the days of their lives, and to *be there* for each other in spirit and in flesh, in body and in soul. It is a commitment in which they state their dedication to this love in good days and in bad; it is a commitment in which they state that if their love lessens and seems about to die, they will remain each other's vocation and will take upon themselves the task of making this love live again. It is a commitment in which they state that their love is above time and will not allow itself to be destroyed by time. And it is a commitment in which they state their conviction that in and through their love they can conquer all of the disintegrating forces which are operative in time. It is obvious that marriage, defined in this way, is quite different from the present concrete institution of marriage in many of its details and in the depth of the ideals on which it is based.

Other Views of Marriage

The definition of marriage given above differs from marriage as popularly understood, and also from marriage as it has been understood until the very recent past by the Catholic church. Since early medieval times, church law has emphasized that marriage is a contract, a binding agreement, which gives to husband and wife certain rights and duties. Foremost among them is the right to sexual intercourse with one's spouse—a right often defined (quite characteristically!) as the right to another's body. In another sense of the word, church law saw marriage as a state, a stable way of life, which resulted from the contract, the prime purpose of which was the procreation and the education of children. Although Paul had urged husbands and wives to love each other, love was strangely absent from the definition of marriage as framed by churchmen and their lawyers. It is true that the "mutual help" of the spouses was admitted as a *secondary* goal of marriage, but this hardly included sexual love, as we have been defining it here.[78] In fact, moral theologians often spoke of intercourse more as a concession which could be tolerated, or as a kind of "bait" to get people to marry and busy themselves with the task of having children. The way of speaking of intercourse was again typical: "remedium concupiscentiae"—a kind of "cure" which one could take in order not to be obsessed with one's drives and fantasies, but a cure which one should strive as far as possible to avoid and which should be used only when absolutely necessary.

However, it is worth noting that neither the Second Vatican Council, nor Paul VI's letter *Humanae Vitae* practices this "legal reductionism." The Council, in fact, refused, not simply to determine the priority of the ends of marriage, but even to speak of the "ends" of marriage at all,[79] and Paul VI preferred in his encyclical to speak of the *meaning* or the *different meanings* of marriage, thereby making his own a position which had been rejected by Pius XII.[80]

Our definition of marriage is also quite different from marriage in the contemporary popular understanding. Beneath much of the romantic rhetoric, marriage is really understood today largely in terms of the mutual satisfaction of needs—primarily emotional and physical needs, and secondarily economic and social needs. The fact that this mutual satisfaction of physical and emotional needs is usually called "love" rests on a serious misunderstanding of what this word really means. Furthermore, in this contemporary understanding of marriage, children are liable to be seen in terms of the satisfactions they bring to their parents, or simply in terms of the fact that they fulfill some deep need of these people to be parents. But the problem with defining marriage and parenthood in terms of needs is that it means that the spouses and children are really being *used* in such an arrangement; however, as we have seen, persons are not to be used but loved. It is also worth noting that when marriage is defined in terms of the mutual satisfaction of needs, it demands neither total commitment nor permanence. In fact, it is nothing more than the commitment to live together, as long as both partners like the arrangement.

Marriage as the Commitment to Sexual Love

Marriage, as an ideal (that is, precisely as *different* from marriage in the popular understanding), has a number of qualities and characteristics which are worth reflecting on. First, it would be seen precisely as a *vocation*, a high calling which no one should undertake lightly. The partners would need to really know each other, and their knowledge would have to be deep enough to justify marital commitment—the act of taking responsibility for this other person through all of his/her life. Such a commitment implies faith and hope in what both partners can become in virtue of a self-transcending sexual love.[81] Such a commitment implies permanence, not because the two need some kind of hold on each other or because they are insecure, but because the commitment involved is *personal*, and in virtue of this fact is a commitment which transcends the limitations of time and is unwilling to subject itself to them. As such, it is the commitment to something in this other person which is not limited by time, and in this regard, it is sacred and it points to the presence of God. It is a commitment which sees sexual love as the revelation of God. Sexual love is, in itself, quite finite and limited, but it is the image and the symbol of that unconditional acceptance which God offers to each of us. (It is for this reason that the Old Testament, particularly in the books of Hosea, Isaiah, and Jeremiah, is able to see marriage as the image and symbol of God's covenant with Israel.)

Marriage as a Sacrament

This is precisely what it means to call marriage a *sacrament*. Sexual love, as we have been defining it, is the *effective sign* of God's love for his people. (It is this insight which lies behind the text in the Epistle to the Ephesians which sees such love as the symbol of the relationship of Christ and the church.) The fact that marriage is a sacrament is rooted in the structure of reality itself. God is the creator of all that is, and all things derive their reality from him. God is the one who decided, in eternity, not to be alone, but to call the world and all who are in it into existence out of nothingness, so that we might share his own being and so that we might love and be loved by him. Everything which exists does so because it participates in God's own being; and because God is the one who decided in eternity not to be alone, the basic law of existence is that all of the things which exist must go outside themselves and find the center and justification of their being in another. Life is a gift, and only the giver is fully alive. This basic law of existence is verified even in the simplest forms of matter. The purely physical effects which material things have on each other are signs of their drive to share their being and to find the center of their existence outside of themselves. Everything which exists seeks to transcend itself in another.

As life takes on more complex forms in the evolutionary process, this basic law of existence is fulfilled more and more completely. For human beings, the drive to find the center of their being in another becomes the power to offer to another the free gift of self; that is, it becomes the power to be there for the other in love. It is our vocation and our destiny to do this as persons, in all of the ways in which our personhood is received and lived. Specifically, we are called to find ourselves by losing ourselves, and to do this in that most profoundly personal form of human existence; that is, in our manly or womanly being. One of the two fundamental ways in which this basic law of existence is manifest in us as persons is called sexual love (in that very special sense in which we have been defining it here: the mutual being-for-each-other of a man and woman on all levels of their existence). This is one of the two basic forms (the other is religious life, as mentioned above) in which the free gift of self is manifest in the fullness of our manly and womanly being, in its spiritual, emotional, and physical dimensions. Everything which exists reveals God in its own way, and sexual love is the fulfillment, in purely inner-worldly terms, of the great mystery that God willed, from eternity, not to be alone. As such, it is the sign and symbol of God's love for the world, and it is the created reality which reveals the mystery of God's love in the midst of our lives.

This is true of marriage, even outside of and apart from Christian faith, and if this were not so, Christian marriage itself could not be a sacrament in the fullest sense of this word. The sacraments are not arbitrary signs which mediate a share in God's life simply because God so willed it. In each of the sacraments, a human and worldly reality which already enjoys its own meaning and possesses its own symbolic power, is taken beyond itself, to point to and effect a new kind of relationship with God. Marriage is an effective sign of God's love for the world--a love which is manifest in his sending of Christ and in the founding of the church--and it is this which keeps marriage, precisely as a commitment to sexual love, from being a purely private matter. It is an act of the church, not primarily because a priest or other representative is there to witness it and record it in the church register. It is an act of the church because the two Christians *who are the real ministers of the sacrament to each other*, are acting here *as church* and are constituting a new community of believers (the family, which will initially be composed of the two of them). Marriage is personal, but it is also public; it is a *covenant* which is a sign of God's covenant with his people, and in making such a covenant, husband and wife are making an intensely personal statement to each other and a very public statement to the whole world.

The Question of Pre-Marital Intercourse

Marriage is obviously no guarantee of sexual love, as we have been defining it, but could it be that marriage and sexual love are so inherently related that sexual love cannot be found apart from marriage? This is one way to raise the question of what is usually called "premarital sex," and even to ask it suggests that, in at least some cases, sexual intercourse before or outside of marriage represents a failure to integrate sexual expression into the total personality and, perhaps surprisingly, might even constitute a failure in sexual love. This is the precise standpoint from which pre-marital sex, at least in some of its forms, ought to be criticized. However, the situation is complex, because it is also clear that at least some of the conduct referred to as premarital sex is motivated by genuine tenderness and concern, and at times would even seem to fulfill the definition of sexual love.

The term "pre-marital sex" is really too vague and ambiguous to be of much use, since it refers to forms of conduct which are objectively different and which spring from very different motives. However, the term is so commonly used that it is probably better to accept it and then carefully define the different forms of conduct to which it can refer and which have to be evaluated in quite different ways.

General Promiscuity

At one extreme, the term "premarital sex" can be used to describe the practice of sleeping around, or engaging in a protracted series of one-night stands. Such behavior is often a sign of severe problems with identity and self-acceptance; and particularly when it is pursued as a form of rebellion, it is only incidentally sexual. But, as we have often noted, sex is not incidental to life and should not be treated as though it were. To make of sexual expression anything other than an act of serious personal commitment is to trivialize sex and this is the same as trivializing ourselves.

At the same time, it is not necessary to over-dramatize the effects of promiscuity. Human beings vary greatly, and some are more capable of real commitment than others. Many people live, by necessity or choice, on a superficial level of life, and they may remain there for most of their lives. Promiscuity on the part of such people probably does relatively little harm to anyone, including themselves, and it is scarcely a matter for righteous indignation. It is true that our sexuality holds great possibilities for making us truly human, and it is true that to put it at the service of anything else is a tragedy, large or small, depending on the circumstances. However, in many cases the real tragedy has taken place at an earlier stage in the lives of those involved, so that they may be simply incapable of living to the full the humanizing mystery of human sexuality. In such cases, the tragedy is not that those who are capable of deep sexual love have chosen to compromise and to act in a way which trivializes sexual expression. The tragedy is that events in childhood or in adolescence have made it virtually impossible for them to achieve sexual love.[82]

Pre-Ceremonial Sex

At the other extreme we have the case of two people who are engaged, formally or informally, but have not yet taken part in a marriage ceremony. Such cases vary considerably, but at least at times, the two appear to be fully committed to each other and intend that commitment to be life-long. In such cases, if the two have sexual relations, it would be better to refer to this as "preceremonial" sex rather than "premarital" sex, because the elements of true marital consent and intent may well be present in their commitment. In such a case, *if* the commitment of the two were so total that neither wanted more time or solitude to review the decision, then the essential element of marital consent would be present, and the argument against sexual union would not be as convincing as it is in other cases, since such union might be the expression of a commitment which they have already made. In any case, it seems obvious that we are dealing with a situation which is objectively worlds apart from that which is mentioned in the preceding section.

However, this situation, as presented here, *may not really be as common as many would like to believe*, except in cases where there is some external obstacle which prevents the marriage (as, for example, the laws in Nazi Germany which prohibited the marriages of "Arians" and Jews, and those in some southern states a generation ago which prohibited interracial marriages). Ordinarily, people think of marriage as beginning with the marriage ceremony, and they feel that marriage has a kind of permanence which engagements do not. In the minds of most of us, the wedding marks the end of the period in which it is possible and appropriate (though perhaps painful) to say, "my commitment is not really total and unrestricted." Two people who love each other should want to safeguard each other's integrity and independence by allowing each other all of the time needed for so important a decision. In this matter, we can deceive ourselves very easily, and unless it is perfectly clear to both parties that the consent given is already marital (permanent and exclusive), it would be better to wait for the integrity of sexual love itself. In such matters, men and women may use the same words and mean something quite different by them, and it can be a shattering experience for the woman involved to find this out.

If marriage were a purely private matter, then in at least some cases it would be difficult to argue that the couple should wait until the ceremony. But marriage is not purely private, and it is the creativity of sexual love in all areas of life which gives it a public dimension. Marriage rests on a hope which no merely human or worldly reality could justify. It is the sign and symbol of the unconditional commitment of God to us human beings. In Christian marriage (and to some degree in all marriages which are solemnized, either religiously, or simply by being registered with the state) the partners are not only making a commitment to each other; they are saying something to the whole world about our human need for total commitment and about the possibility of making such a commitment, against all odds. The world *needs* to hear them make such a statement and the world *has a right* to learn of such a commitment. In sexual love we are totally *for* each other, and it is precisely for that reason that we have something of inestimable value to say to family, friends, acquaintances, and to the world at large. No man or woman is an island; our successes and our failures are personal but not private, because in them we touch each other and the world at large.

This is a point which we ought to keep in mind when we discuss the possibility of "living together" without a marriage ceremony. Although many people mean, in using this ambiguous term, simply enjoying a sexual relationship which neither partner intends to last, at least some people live together with the desire of staying together more or less indefinitely. They seem to feel that the genuinity of their commitment would not be helped by marriage but rather hindered (and they may have come to this conclusion by observing the marriages of their friends or of members of their families). They may also have decided that they are not capable of permanent commitment at this moment in their lives (or this may simply be a bit of trendy rhetoric they have picked up while listening to the omnipresent psycho-babble of our day). To be incapable of permanent commitment is a sign of a by no means trivial personality disorder. But if people are really incapable of such commitment, then we can admit that "living together" might be the lesser of two evils and might even be a tolerable solution to a real problem. But this situation may really not be too common. In most "living together" arrangements the two probably want to delay the question of permanent commitment while enjoying themselves; but there are dangers here, too. The woman involved is probably, whether she likes to admit it or not, much more interested in making the relation permanent than her partner is; and so there is real danger that their sexual expression, which should be the expression of *love*, will become, while remaining quite pleasurable, a sly way of using and manipulating each other for purposes which they do not share. Sooner or later they realize this, and when they break up, the capacities of each for true sexual love will not have grown but will have diminished. It is from this standpoint that such arrangements merit serious criticism.

The Difficult Case

Between the extremes of promiscuity on the one hand and genuine marital consent on the other, there is a third possibility which is itself not a single definable form of conduct, but covers a rather broad spectrum of cases which range over the whole middle ground between the two extremes. The case we are considering now could be described this way: a man and woman are drawn to each other, enjoy each other's company, feel real affection for each other, and in some sense they even love each other. But for various reasons they are not even thinking of making a permanent commitment to each other. Sexual intercourse may seem to them to be a good and proportionate expression of their affection and their love.

This situation is more common today than in the past, not because of any really deep change in sexual customs and values, but because of the availability of more effective and esthetically less objectionable contraceptives. Christians encounter this situation as do others, and they often enough decide in favor of sexual relations under these circumstances. Many are somewhat troubled in conscience by what they are doing, but they feel that the traditional teaching of their churches in this matter is uncertain enough (or unrealistic enough) to justify their conduct. They have found just enough sympathy for their views, even among Catholic moral theologians, that Rome has found it necessary on several occasions during the past fifteen years to reaffirm the traditional Catholic position on the sinfulness of extramarital sex. Of course, the mere fact that more liberal views have become common does not make them correct; but it does suggest that it might be a good idea to reexamine the traditional views and to ask if they might still be correct, but for different and better reasons than those which are usually given.

It does seem clear that Christians and their churches have overreacted to this problem in the past and continue to do this even today, and this is probably even more often the case with Catholics than with Protestants. In dealing with the question of premarital sex, Christians have often reacted with righteous indignation, threats of hell-fire, and a single-minded obsession with physical virginity. Reactions like this are not really justified by the New Testament; they are unfortunate remnants of tabuistic thinking and they should have no place in a genuinely Christian discussion. We should be able to speak calmly of a particular way of acting and we should be able to note that it is often ill-advised and may work in a serious way against genuine human sexual fulfillment, but we should be able to do this without becoming overwrought and without acting as though failure in this matter were the ultimate and irremediable human tragedy.

I believe that it is a mistake to present the issue of premarital sex (in any form) as one which can be resolved *simply* by applying the law of God—either the natural law or divine positive law. Law, as generally understood, is a poor basis on which to construct a genuinely Christian ethical code. The traditional natural law arguments against sexual intercourse for those who are in love but do not yet share a real marital commitment have been very much weakened by the availability of contraceptives (obviously a much-debated point—see the next chapter). Furthermore, the New Testament does not address this issue directly; references to extramarital sex (usually called fornication) occur almost entirely in the context of prostitution. Jesus never addressed the issue as such, but it is evident that he associated with people who had a poor track record in matters of sexual purity.

I believe that it is not entirely accurate to assert that sexual relations in the case under discussion are always exploitative, selfish, and lustful. Anyone who talks to people who are involved in such a relationship knows that this is often not the case. Furthermore, some of the arguments used against premarital sex in the case of those who are in some sense in love but not yet ready to marry seemed to suggest that the same act (intercourse) was bad before the wedding, but became good (or at least tolerable) after the ceremony. This really makes no sense and attributes a magical character to the marriage ceremony—a character which is hardly Christian. The real point at issue is not whether the ceremony has the power to transform guilty sex into not-guilty sex; the real point at issue is whether full sexual expression (intercourse), calls, of its own very nature, for an exclusive and permanent commitment. If it does, then the marriage ceremony, although far from irrelevant, is not really the issue at all.

To view the question of sex before marriage in this way implies that from the standpoint of sexual love as an ideal, sexual relationships without permanent commitment have some serious shortcomings, all of which are rooted in the fact that such relationships more often than not conspire against the fullness and integrity of sexual love itself. There is an unrestrictedness in sexual intercourse, a total openness of man and woman to each other in this situation, which make it a fitting and fully appropriate expression of the total commitment of a man and a woman to each other. Sexual intercourse without this commitment is not saying what it *can* say and is not saying what it *should* say.

But there is a much more important side to this. The unrestricted commitment of a man and woman to each other is a truly splendid thing. It is the commitment *to be there* for this other person in all dimensions of one's being. As a decision, it is an achievement of the human mind and spirit, but because we are not pure spirits, this decision needs to be symbolized and realized in bodily expression. For much of our lives, sexual intercourse provides this symbol and this bodily expression. But if sexual intercourse has already been used to symbolize and express something else (affection, concern, caring, a love which is real but falls short of permanent commitment), then there is no way left to symbolize and realize a commitment which is total and permanent. The desire to find an outlet for sexual energy is powerful, and its roots are deep, but the desire to find another, to whom we can give ourselves without reserve, has roots which are deeper still; and unless our sexual energy is an expression of this transcendence, sought and found, we will never find joy and abiding peace.[83]

But this is precisely the problem: will we find this joy and peace? If tentativeness has been deified and if sexual expression has too often been used to say "I enjoy you" to someone for whom we have no intention of either living or dying, we may not. The answer depends on many things, and not least on the age of those involved. A very important part of the process of growing up is coming to see the enormous humanizing possibilities of true sexual love, but early experimentation with the more superficial levels of sexual expression by those without much emotional maturity may very well inhibit this process. The sexes are made for each other, and yet there are many areas in which the sad misunderstanding of the sexes for each other can do serious harm. Sexual relations during early adolescence certainly come under this heading. There is more than a little truth to the dictum of popular wisdom, that boys want sex and will give affection to get it, and that girls want affection and will give sex to get it. The problem with such trade-offs is that they may blind both to the fact that in an authentically human sexual relationship, sexual expression, affection, and love form an indissoluble unity.[84]

However, it is obvious that today a much larger percentage of both men and women have had sexual relations before marriage than was the case even thirty years ago, and the proportional increase in premarital sexual relations among Catholics is even greater. Many sincere and committed Catholics find that this has been their experience, and they do not necessarily think that they acted wrongly or made a mistake in acting as they did. They seem to feel that sexual relations played an appropriate role in their lives before marriage, and that it is *marriage itself* (not simply the ceremony, but the permanent state) which is the sign of their permanent commitment to this other person on all levels of their being. The experience of honest and sincere people should not be discounted, but it is still reasonable to ask if this view or theory is not being adopted as a kind of "consolation prize," in the attempt to find something of ultimate value which can symbolize total commitment to the other, when sexual intercourse has been used to say something else. Sexual expression *should* be a sign of the love which is constitutive of the marital state, and it has the power to function as a sign in a way in which marriage itself does not.

But if premarital sex in any of the cases under discussion here (those who like each other but are not ready for permanent commitment) can interfere with sexual love and true marital commitment, is the damage irreparable? Of course it is not. In life we are continually acting in ways which are more or less harmful and which hurt others as well as ourselves. It would be better if we did not act in this way, but Christian faith affirms that to those who do act this way, the love and acceptance of God are always offered. But we can only receive this love if we want it and we will always receive it as forgiveness. If we try to solve the problem of guilt by pretending that we have done no wrong, then and only then will our guilt destroy us. We can refuse to let God be the one who loves us and we do this by refusing to face the real nature of the choices which we have made. The mistakes which we make in regard to our sexuality are irreparable only when we keep insisting that they are not mistakes. The marvel of Christian existence is that even mistakes can be integrated into life and can promote the attainment of real marital, sexual love.

To summarize: as human beings we need commitment and, difficult though it is, we need a commitment which is permanent, total, and all-absorbing. For most human beings, sexual love should be the form which this commitment takes. When it does, physical sexual expression becomes a deeply human and humanizing reality. When physical sex is not a sign of this kind of commitment, then, although it is addictive, it seems to lose its power to be deeply satisfying and to bring us joy and peace. Instead, it turns to bizarre and impersonal ways of showing itself, either in marriage or outside of it. When sexual expression is true to its own inner dynamisms, it is a creative and humanly fulfilling experience, the only alternative to which is a unique personal relationship with God which has strong mystical overtones. In the absence of both of these, life will be empty indeed.

Marriage: Ideal and Reality

Sacramental marriage, as described in this chapter is a very high ideal. It is an ideal which can be reached only by people who are aware that it *is* such an ideal, and who know that, paradoxically, it must be actively sought and at the same time accepted as pure gift, both from God and from the loved one. It may take many years before anything like this ideal can be attained in a marriage, but unless it is dimly envisaged at the beginning, a man and woman will have little or no idea of what they are called upon to do and to be, and failure is virtually guaranteed. It is the task of married people to live out this ideal and in doing so to be a sign to all, inside the church and outside it, that nothing is impossible for God and for those who rely on his help.

Even while admiring this ideal, we have to face the fact that very many marriages are going to fall short of it, and that in a number of marriages, whether they are celebrated in church or not, neither of the partners have any idea of what Christian marriage really means, nor will they ever learn, in the course of their entire lives together. As human beings we fail at marriage, as we do in all other areas of life. Some of these failed marriages continue "til death does them part," either because of inertia or because of the conventionalism of the partners; many more end in divorce, and this is happening today much more frequently than in the past. Divorce is a serious problem today, particularly for Catholics, precisely because it poses a threat to the ideal of sexual love in marriage, while at the same time it is an inevitable and therefore necessary means of coping with the fact that marriages do fail.

Divorce

Although this may seem to be an exaggeration, I believe that it would be true to say that a marriage which is truly a mutual commitment to sexual love, as we have been defining it, *cannot fail,* because, come what may, the partners *will not allow it to fail.* Their commitment to each other and to the bond which makes them man and wife partakes of that hope which rings in the words of Gabriel Marcel: "To say 'I love you' is to say 'You will not die.'" Marriages which do fail were not, despite the good will and good faith of the participants, the proclamation of that kind of commitment. It will be easier to cope with the problem of divorce and to find some solutions which recognize both the ideal and the reality of marriage, if we try to describe the nature of a marriage which was not a mutual commitment, in faith and hope, to remain each other's vocation for as long as they both live.

Marriage as a Limited Commitment

It is important to note that the kind of marriage which this odd title describes is not necessarily a failed marriage (irrespective of whether the parties separate), at least in the eyes of husband and wife. Many people apparently don't know of anything better and don't really understand what sexual love means. Many are quite content with the satisfactions which are offered by marriage as a limited commitment; if both feel this way, the situation is not too tragic, and is simply a sign that unfortunate events in childhood or adolescence have somehow blinded them to the humanizing mystery of sexual love, or that circumstances in life prevented their finding a truly suitable marriage partner. If only one of the partners is satisfied with comfortable mediocrity and the other was really committed to the quest for sexual love and total commitment, then the latter has a real cross to bear, and even divorce is going to be an unsatisfying solution.

Marriage as a limited commitment could be described in this way: it is a legally binding contract to live together and to share "bed and board." It is a contract which defines the rights, duties, and responsibilities of the partners to each other and to any children they might have. Despite some residual rhetoric in the marriage vows, both partners in such a marriage know that they really did not intend their union to be permanent; they were agreeing to live together just as long as both of them preferred the arrangement to any other alternative.

Without being overly cynical, we might note that the majority of people in this country (and at least a significant minority of Catholics) have something like this in mind when they marry. They think of marriage as a way of living together which is approved by society. Their reasons for entering such a marriage are varied, but they almost always involve the satisfaction of a number of needs. Sometimes these needs are primarily sexual and emotional. Often the elements of security and respectability are strong. Sometimes, especially for older people, the need for congenial companionship may be paramount.

None of these needs really demand sexual love in the true sense of the word, although there may be real affection in many of these cases. And none of these needs really demand permanence, precisely because they are needs which can be satisfied without personal love. But we should mention an interesting possibility that probably is realized at least occasionally. A marriage might start off on this level of limited commitment, and then, either because one or both of the partners reached a level of emotional maturity which they did not have at the time of the wedding, or because of some shaking experience which revealed possibilities which they had not suspected, the relationship might grow into one of real sexual love. When this happens, it comes about because one or both of the partners have made some basic choices for God and neighbor in other areas of life and have come to sense possibilities in the marital relationship which they did not see before, and this is a truly wonderful event.

Marriage as a limited commitment is not necessarily tragic. In many situations, the highest human ideal may not be attainable, although some measure of human satisfaction and fulfillment may be, and so there is nothing wrong with choosing the limited good which is attainable. Such compromises are part of life, and they are tragic only when they are chosen by those who are capable of much more.

Divorce as a Catholic Problem

Divorce presents very serious problems for Catholics, because according to the teaching of church authorities for at least the last millenium, every marriage which has been validly contracted between Christians and which has been consummated *after* the wedding, is automatically a sacrament, and can be dissolved only by the death of one of the parties. This position has strong New Testament roots, both in Mark's Gospel and in the Epistle to the Ephesians, where the marital relationship is regarded as an image of the relationship of Christ and the church. Although certain ways of stating the Catholic position were unduly harsh, the position itself is solidly based in the New Testament and the scriptural foundation of the indissolubility of the marriage bond is much broader than merely the two texts cited. It is part of the very substance of the Old and New Testament revelation. Truly sacramental marriages may be the exception rather than the rule, but there is no doubt that they constitute the scriptural ideal. They are made in time, but they are the earthly symbol of the eternal love of God; for this reason, they are immune to the ravages of time, and they demand that we acknowledge this immunity.

Jesus' words on the subject of divorce are given both by Mark and by Matthew. Although in the text of Mark, Jesus seems to prohibit divorce without any exception, most of the translations of Matthew imply that adultery would constitute grounds for divorce. In this matter, Catholics used to appeal to Mark, and Protestants (who, for historical reasons, tended to be somewhat more lenient on this matter) relied on Matthew, and there were many lively debates on whether Mark or Matthew gave us the "very words of Jesus." The development of critical methods of interpretation has led to a great measure of agreement among competent exegetes of all confessions. They agree that Mark brings us closer to the point which Jesus was really making, and that Matthew has edited Jesus' words, to bring them into line with the Jewish law on impediments to marriage. (It is quite probable that the word which has been translated as "adultery" does not mean this at all, but actually refers to marriages which had been contracted among pagans but which were within the degree of consanguinity which was prohibited by Jewish law.) In any case, it is foolish to interpret Jesus' words as though he intended to legislate on the questions of marriage and divorce. Here, as in all similar cases, Jesus' words are not law; they are a statement of what is possible for those who really know the gift of God which is being offered. The demand is first of all a gift and it remains a gift, even when expressed as a summons and a call (and in *this* sense of the word, a demand). Jesus did not say that those who remarry should be excluded from the sacramental life of the church; and to assert that it is not a good thing for a marriage to break up is not the same thing as to demand sexual abstinence from guilty and innocent alike until the end of their days.

However, this was the way in which Jesus' words have been interpreted. The prohibition of divorce was so strict that when Catholics did obtain a civil divorce and then remarried, they were excommunicated (banned from the church and the sacraments) and were considered to be "living in sin." This ordinarily meant that no church burial would be allowed when they died; and if they came from strict Catholic families, it might mean that they would be ostracized by their closest relatives. If they wanted to return to the church and the sacraments, they were told that there were only two possibilities: either they were to separate from their present partners (in the second marriage), or, if this was impossible (because children had been born to them) they would have to promise to "live as brother and sister"; that is, sexual relations were absolutely prohibited, on the grounds that the second marriage, not recognized by the church, did not really exist, and therefore sexual relations would constitute adultery.

The "Internal Forum" Solution

This rigid legislation was in effect from the medieval period up to about 1962. At that time, a new practice began to be introduced into a number of dioceses with the tacit approval of Rome, and this practice spread quite rapidly after 1966. It is known as the *internal forum* solution, because it did not fit in well with the public law of the church and because it was offered by the priest in the framework of confession. The way it worked was as follows: divorced and remarried Catholics who requested it (in the context of confession), could be readmitted to the sacraments and would be permitted to live together with their new spouses (that is, sexual relations were permitted) provided no scandal was given (that is, provided that their conduct would not be interpreted by others as implying that the church sanctioned divorce and remarriage). Usually the husband and wife were told to quietly explain to their families and friends what had happened (and they were reminded that they were still responsible for any obligations which they had incurred during the first marriage: child support, alimony, etc.). The general assumption behind this new policy seems to have been this: those who requested a return to the sacraments were not responsible for the break-up of the first marriage (or were less responsible than the other spouse) and, in any case, the first marriage was beyond hope of repair. It was also assumed that the partners to the second marriage had acted in good faith and that they did not see their decision to remarry as sinful. (This second assumption was made possible by the growing awareness of the importance of the distinction between ontic evil and moral evil, an awareness which was gaining ground in the church at the time.) At the same time, no official recognition was given to the second marriage; it was simply "there"—a fact which did not fit in at all well with the official theory of what marriage was, or with canon law on marriage. The official teaching on the indissolubility of marriage did not change at all. Despite occasional rumblings from Rome, this practice continues in effect today, and in many dioceses and parishes there is official recognition given to the apostolate to divorced and remarried Catholics.

Annulments

Divorce, in the proper sense of the word, has not been allowed to Catholics in the Western Church for the past thousand years; but it is allowed to members of the Orthodox churches of the East today, and it was occasionally tolerated in the West during part of the first thousand years. However, several things which looked like divorce have been allowed in the church and are approved today. These are worthy of brief mention now for two reasons: first, they will give us some understanding of why the church took the position it did on various problems connected with the indissolubility of marriage, and second, one of these "things which looked like divorce" has undergone remarkable development during the past twenty years and has resulted in the termination of many "things which looked like marriage" between Catholics.

Church teaching has always been that a marriage which was performed in the proper way (witnessed by a priest who acted as official representative of the church) but which had not been consummated *after* the marriage ceremony, was not yet fully and definitively sacramental, and could therefore be dissolved by the church. The case was relatively rare, but it might occur, for example, when the groom deserted the bride at the door of the church, because he had gone through the ceremony merely "to give the child a name." However, if the couple had been together for anything more than three minutes in any place more private than a telephone booth, it was assumed that they had had intercourse and therefore that the marriage was indissoluble.

In addition to this relatively rare case, church law had always asserted that there were various possible defects in the marriage ceremony itself, which might prevent it from being a true marriage, despite appearances. For example, church law stated that the marriage of Catholics had to take place in the presence of a priest as the official witness of the church; if Catholics attempted marriage before a civil official or a Protestant minister, the marriage was not recognized as valid (that is, as a real marriage) by Catholic authorities. In addition, church law had stated (since the medieval period) that marriage was a contract and that it could be entered into only with the free consent of both parties. If either or both parties gave their consent only under the threat of physical force or under some other kind of psychological pressure, then it was agreed that, despite appearances, no marriage had taken place.

In addition to these cases, church authorities claimed the right, in principle, to dissolve certain non-sacramental marriages (those in which at least one of the parties was non-Christian), and they have exercised this right on a number of occasions in order to allow second marriages to church members. The best-known example of such a process is the so-called "Pauline Privilege," although there are two other similar cases which are usually grouped together and referred to as the "Petrine Privilege." The essential point in all these cases is that the marriage dissolved had not taken place between two Christians, and was therefore not a sacrament.

In both the non-consummated marriage and the apparent marriage in which there was some kind of defect in the ceremony or the contract, church authorities had always been willing, at least in theory, to grant an *annulment*— that is, a declaration that, despite appearances, no marriage had actually taken place. When such an annulment was granted, church authorities always insisted that the parties get a civil divorce (in countries where this was possible), in order to take care of the civil effects of the terminated (apparent) marriage. There was much connected with the granting of these annulments which constituted a real scandal: all of these cases had to go to Rome and they often were settled only after many years. It took money to get an annulment (or to speed up the process), and therefore, in practice, they were reserved to the rich and the powerful.

Up until about twenty years ago, annulments would be granted (after the expenditure of much time and money) if there was cogent evidence that no marriage had taken place, but there was a strong presumption in law in favor of the validity of the marriage, and the burden of proof rested on those who contested its validity. The reason for this was that the marriage bond (that is, the marriage itself) was regarded as a sacred thing, and was not to be trifled with or taken lightly. This attitude was often criticized on the grounds that it placed the law, or a juridical fact, on a higher level than the persons who sought to be released from an impossible situation. However, this criticism was really unfair, because the purpose of the law was to protect the integrity of marriage for the sake of the real people who entered into this state. There were serious problems with the practice of annulments, but they were due to other factors, principally financial in nature.

Just after 1970, annulment practice in the church began to change in some important ways, with the result that many more annulments are being granted today.[85] Interestingly enough, the *reasons* for granting annulments have not changed at all, but there have been great changes in methods of evaluating the evidence in order to determine whether or not the parties were *free* when they apparently contracted matrimony.

Before 1970, annulments were granted only when there was some *public* knowledge of the fact that one or both of the parties were not free, and where reputable witnesses were willing to swear that either or both of the parties had married under duress or coercion. Since about 1970, church authorities have taken a much broader view of the factors which can limit free choice and which therefore might prevent an act from being performed with the knowledge and deliberation required for true freedom. Before 1970 it was generally felt that anyone who was not a certifiable psychopath had the requisite freedom. Today it is recognized that there are many factors which may lead to temporary mental unbalance and that immaturity itself is a factor which may severely limit the ability of the individual to perform a free act. Another very important aspect of the whole annulment question is that today these cases are not automatically sent to Rome for adjudication. They are handled on the diocesan level (and then checked on the regional level) and the whole process may take little more than a year, and sometimes less.

Typical questions which are asked in annulment cases are these: Was there any noticeable lack of stability or mental balance on the part of either party? At the time of the marriage, was either one under psychological pressure or emotional strain? Was either one emotionally immature? Did they rush into marriage quickly, in a way which suggests that it was not a considered decision? Was either using marriage as an escape from some other situation (such as an unhappy life at home with parents)? At the time of the wedding, did either have serious doubts about whether marriage was really the right choice?

These new annulments are not easy to evaluate from a Christian point of view. They have done some good and they have done some harm. They have provided an acceptable way out of "marriages" which were nothing more than silly mistakes, but at the same time, the modern annulment is rapidly becoming the "Catholic way of divorce." The grounds for annulment are really quite broad, and, in practice if not in theory, they can become simply a way of saying that the two people in question were not aware, before the wedding, of how totally incompatible they were. In all honesty, it would seem that many of these annulments are really divorces, as any reasonable person understands that term; and, like all divorces which come after protestations of lifelong commitment or eternal love, they do some harm (although they may be better than any available alternative). To assert that divorce is, at least usually, not a good thing, and to note that it always implies a degree of guilt, often on the part of both husband and wife, is not to make it the end of the world. Certainly divorce is sometimes better than "staying together for the sake of the children," because the unspoken and suppressed tensions in such an arrangement can often do great harm, especially to the children. Despite all of the problems connected with divorce, in many cases it is probably better for two people to face the fact that their marriage is unsavable and to do whatever is necessary to minimize the harm done to innocent bystanders. After this, it should be possible for the two to start over again with new partners, perhaps a little less starry-eyed, but somewhat wiser for the experience. Annulment, as the "Catholic way of divorce" makes this possible, but it does so at the price of making it very easy to nullify a commitment to another person which everyone, including the persons in question, thought they were making. Divorce is a problem, because when it comes to be regarded as acceptable this leads to a general doubt about whether a permanent commitment on the part of two human beings to lifelong sexual love is possible. Divorce is, at best, an unfortunate necessity; this is what the New Testament says, directly and indirectly, and this is what the church should preach. However, if we preach the unconditional demands of Jesus, then we have to preach his unconditional acceptance as well.

Some Final Observations on Marriage

Marriage is the commitment of two people to sexual love and thus to a love which touches all levels of their existence. It is a commitment which lays claim to that which is deepest in them as persons. It is *their* commitment, and although it is important that they make this commitment in the presence of God and God's people (the church), nothing should obscure the fact that it is their commitment, and that all of the others who are there—priest, parents, friends—are there as witnesses.

Social and family pressures often conspire to conceal this truth from all participants, including the bride and the groom. The event of getting married is thus often turned into a traumatic experience which dedicates an inordinate amount of money to a show which nobody really enjoys. The occasion of getting married should be one of great seriousness and great joy, but it is often turned into a public-relations hype job which neither the bride nor the groom really want, although they may be only dimly aware of this.

In summary, in the church we should preach the ideal of sexual love and promote it as a very high vocation. We should state much more clearly than we have that the real ministers of the sacrament of matrimony are the bride and groom and not the priest. The church should affirm that marriage, as the formation of a new community within the church by two who are members of the church, has a public character, and those who undertake to form such a community should voice their commitment at the liturgy in the place where they usually celebrate it. In those sad cases where what seemed to be a real commitment to sexual love turned out to be a bad mistake, the church should let the parties start over again with other spouses, without any public proclamation in church, but without telling them that they are in serious sin and without refusing them a share in the sacramental life of the church. In other words, the "internal forum solution" should be made available. Annulments would probably then decline in number; there would be a great gain in all-around honesty, and Christian marriage could remain a splendid but not unreal ideal—the earthly sign of Christ's love for the Church and God's love for the world.

7.

The Problem of Contraception

The question of contraception or, as it is often called, artificial birth control, is obviously not one which concerns only married people; but it does pose moral problems of a somewhat different nature for the married and the unmarried. For the sake of clarity it will be better to examine the question as it relates to married people and then touch the question of contraceptive practice by the unmarried in a brief note at the conclusion.

Up until the early 1960's the question of whether or not to practice birth control was often presented (in premarital counselling and in sermons directed to married people) as the most important moral problem confronting Catholic married couples. But today, for better or for worse, this is no longer being done; the majority of Catholic married couples have rejected the teaching of church authorities in this matter, and few priests are trying to change the mind of married people on this question. The issue of birth control may be more important today, not as an issue of sexual morality, but because it raises the question of authority, specifically the authority of papal teaching in moral matters.

(Here, as in other areas, the fact that even an overwhelming majority of people differ with the traditional teaching, does not necessarily mean that the traditional teaching is wrong or should be revised. But it does mean, particularly when many of those who disagree seem to be quite serious about their faith, that the traditional teaching and the arguments used to support it should be reexamined with care.)

Traditional Papal Teaching on Contraception

The official teaching was formulated by Pius XI and Pius XII, between 1930 and 1958. To some extent, their views drew on the work of moral theologians in the early modern period (the sixteenth and seventeenth centuries), but these early discussions were very academic, simply because the mass production of even moderately effective contraceptives is a twentieth-century phenomenon. John XXIII (1958 to 1962) really had nothing to say about the question, but the traditional position was affirmed by Paul VI (1962 to 1978, but above all in his encyclical, *Humanae Vitae,* in 1968) and, though less formally, by John Paul II in recent years.

According to this papal teaching, although it might be permissible to limit the number of one's children, only one method (short of total abstinence) was allowed—the so-called "rhythm" method, or periodic continence. [86] This method consists in limiting intercourse to times when the wife is unlikely to conceive. On the other hand, all other methods of birth control were described as "artificial" and were prohibited under pain of serious sin. These other methods included the use of mechanical means: diaphragms, condoms, IUD's (intra-uterine devices), as well as spermicidal sprays and contraceptive pills.

The arguments used by the previously mentioned Popes in their encyclicals (public letters to the whole church) and their allocutions (addresses directed to special groups, but intended to present authentic papal teaching) are not based on scripture, but on *natural law*—a term which, for them, meant "the necessary and universal structures of human life and activity." (The Popes themselves acknowledged this, but the very fact that the argument is, for this reason, not strictly theological, but philosophical in character, raises some interesting questions about why it has played so prominent a role in papal teaching during the last fifty years.) This natural law argument against what has been called "artificial birth control" can be summarized in four steps, and no matter what position one eventually takes on the question, it is important to appreciate the structure of this argument and, granted certain presuppositions, its cogency.

First, sexual intercourse is a natural, biological process. Here the word "natural" refers to a way of acting which has its own inherent purpose; that is, its purpose is "given" in the nature of the case and it is not up to us to determine it. To call the process "biological" is simply to assert that its purpose is determined by the need to propagate or protect life, physical life. Note carefully that the papal teaching does not deny that intercourse is, or at least should be, *more* than a merely biological process. It simply asserts that whatever else sexual intercourse may be on some occasions (or ought to be on all occasions), of its very nature it is always, and at least, a biological process.

Second, this process is obviously designed to move to a certain term and to achieve a certain purpose. The whole reproductive mechanism is designed to bring two cells, the ovum and the sperm, together. Sexual excitement adapts the organs themselves for intercourse, in the process of which the sperm is given a path to seek out the ovum. To summarize, sexual intercourse is obviously designed to secure fertilization of the ovum by a sperm cell.

Third, it is possible to interfere with this process. This can be done by mechanical means (condoms, diaphragms, IUD's), by pharmaceutical means (spermicidal jellies and sprays, or, on a somewhat different level, the pill), or simply by withdrawal of the penis before the ejaculation of sperm. Since it seems clear that fertilization normally occurs in the fallopian tubes, it may be that some of the pharmaceutical methods actually function by preventing *implantation* of the already fertilized ovum, and not by preventing fertilization itself. There is no firm agreement on the part of moral theologians on how to handle this case, but many of them tend to argue that the number of fertilized ova which do *not* implant in the uterus is far greater than the number which do, and that therefore *human* life should be thought of as beginning, not with fertilization, but with implantation.

Fourth, it is seriously wrong to frustrate a fundamental process which is part of our very nature. To violate a life-process in this way is to violate human life itself and to destroy the finality, the purposiveness, of sexual intercourse. This is the case, not because the sperm is killed, but because the awakening of new life is deliberately blocked. Note that according to the traditional position of the Popes mentioned above, contraception is a *serious matter* (that is, matter for mortal sin) precisely because reproduction is a fundamental necessity and the passing on of life is a sacred duty. Note also that in this traditional position, it is precisely the *interference* from the outside which is wrong. If sexual intercourse fails to result in fertilization because of some "natural" fact or event (for example, if intercourse occurs after menopause or during that time of the month when the ovum is not correctly placed for fertilization), there is no moral problem at all (at least in modern times; Augustine and the overwhelming majority of medieval moral theologians would have been scandalized by this view). In fact, assuming that there is a good reason for not wanting a child at that particular time, Catholic teaching in modern times has allowed and even encouraged couples to take advantage of the wife's infertile period and to have intercourse during that time. It has been regarded as permissible to calculate the time and duration of the infertile period, using body temperature, smear tests, and other such means to determine it as exactly as possible, and Pius XII urged doctors and researchers to perfect such methods.

Other Views on Contraception

The traditional Catholic position summarized above makes some very strong points. It is based on the conviction that human nature is knowable, at least in its essentials, and that there are goals and purposes inherent in life which must not be violated. At the same time, it is not unreasonable to examine the arguments given in the preceding section, and to ask if they have taken all of the data into account. Doubts about the cogency of these arguments have been voiced rather widely in the church during the past twenty-five years. The official papal teaching has not changed and gives no sign of changing now, but it has not been accepted by a majority of the laity for whom it is a living issue, and a large number of priests seem no longer to accept it. There were a number of bishops who wanted to see the question opened up at the Second Vatican Council (1962-1965), but Paul VI would not allow it to be discussed by the bishops, and appointed a commission which was to report to him after the Council was over. It seems obvious that most of the bishops who called for discussion of the question were convinced that some changes should be made in the official teaching on birth control. What this means is that there are several groups in the church today, including at least a significant minority of the hierarchy, who are not really satisfied with papal teaching from 1930 to the present on the question of birth control. The reasons for this malaise are diverse, but we will not be far off the mark if we attempt to summarize them under these three points.

First, although it is clear that sexual intercourse is a natural biological process, nevertheless the real nature of human sexual intercourse may be more complex than the traditional position has been willing to admit. It is true that the official Catholic position has never denied that sexual intercourse between human beings may and should be more than simply a biological act, but it has affirmed that, whatever else it is, its natural biological character must not be destroyed. At least in this sense, the traditional position argues that the natural and biological character of intercourse is a central and essential element; however, this is the very point which honest and open reflection on the human condition does not find easy to support today. Many who call for a rethinking of traditional Catholic teaching ask if it is really true that the central and essential element of human sexual intercourse is that which it appears to have in common with mating behavior in the rest of the animal kingdom. The argument can be made that in the human being, intelligence, personality, and humanity itself are not simply added to an animal nature which is already in possession of its own meaning and purpose. Our "animality" is not self-contained; it does not derive its meaning from the various purposes which are proper to the rest of the animal world, but from something which utterly transcends that world—namely personal love. Against this point, it is sometimes asserted that even when human finality transcends that of the animal functions of nature, nevertheless it should not frustrate or destroy them, but incorporate them into human finality; and, in principle, this is by no means a trivial point. However, this argument may beg the question, for a reason that is rarely noted. It is questionable that human sexuality, *even in its physical entity,* is really identical with the sexuality of the other animals. This point is not only extremely important, but it also touches the other points in this brief summary; for this reason, we will look at it, after they have been discussed.

Second, those who have reservations about papal teaching agree that sexual intercourse, if viewed from a truly human perspective, is designed to move toward a certain term and to achieve a certain result. But a significant number of Catholic theologians today point out that this term and result is not precisely the conception of a child (obviously not in every act of intercourse), but rather the *fostering and promoting, the symbolizing and realizing of marital, sexual love.* This love is, like all true love, fruitful and productive of new life. When conditions make it appropriate, marital love will be fruitful by bringing a child into the world. When conditions do not make this appropriate, marital love will still be fruitful, precisely in all of the ways in which sexual love is fruitful (which we saw when we spoke of the creativity of sexual love).

Third, Catholics who question the traditional position on contraception agree that it is possible to interfere with sexual intercourse in such a way as to keep it from attaining its proper goal and purpose. But rather than limiting this interference to mechanical and pharmaceutical means, they tend to argue that there are serious problems with the one method of birth control which has won church approval (the rhythm method) on precisely this score. Traditional Catholic opposition to birth control has been based on the assumption that it used methods which were *artificial,* because they were means of human meddling in a divinely ordered process. But there may be another kind of artificiality in the rhythm method itself. A number of women who have written about the rhythm method allude to its unreliability,[87] which introduces an element of anxiety into the marital relationship. They also point out that it is likely to demand abstinence at precisely those times when the desire of physical sexual expression may be strongest on the part of both husband and wife. Some have spoken of an unnatural programming of their emotional lives which introduces tension into the marital relationship.[88]

The Purpose of Human Sexuality on the Physical, Biological Level

The so-called "natural law" argument against contraception is based, in large part, on the intrinsic finality and purposiveness of sexual intercourse as a biological phenomenon. As we noted, defenders of papal teaching never deny that human sexual intercourse should be *more* than this, but they also argue that it should never be *less*—that is, that the intrinsic finality of intercourse on the physical and biological level should not be negated—and this view is strongly reasserted in *Humanae Vitae*.[89] This raises a question which has not been given much attention: the question of whether human sexuality even in its biological dimensions, is really the same as sexuality in the rest of the animal world.

The other functions which we share with our animal relatives—eating and drinking are good examples—are essentially the same, on the physical and biological level, when performed by human beings or the other animals. And this remains true, even though eating can and should have a social function for us—that is, it should be a sign of the acceptance and affirmation of those who share the food with us. However, even on the physical and biological level, human sexual intercourse is *not* essentially the same as sexual intercourse among the other animals. In the course of evolution, adaptations arose in the very physical nature of human sexuality which have had a profound effect on the role of sexual expression in human life and on the preservation of the human community. Although there are variations in sexual desire which follow the menstrual cycle, a woman is essentially sexually receptive throughout the year, and therefore human couples are drawn to sexual activity with a frequency which has no real relation to the possible conception of children. To put it another way, it would seem to be quite *natural* for human sexual intercourse, because of evolutionary developments in human biology, *not* to result in conception but rather to serve other purposes—for example, the building of stable, monogamous relationships which came to be very important for the rearing of those children who were already born. I believe that this fact should weigh heavily in any rethinking of the traditional position of the church on contraception.

Birth Control and the Unmarried

A generation ago, a number of moral theologians taught that if unmarried people used contraceptives during intercourse, they were committing two serious sins, compounding the evil of extra-marital intercourse with the evil of contraceptive practice (although privately many of these same theologians admitted that the motive of not wanting to bring a child into the world in such inherently unstable conditions was a good one). Today it is safe to say that, regardless of their attitude toward premarital sex as such, most moral theologians would urge those engaging in it to use contraceptives. However, attitudes here are very ambivalent, and they surface almost every day in the ongoing discussion about supplying contraceptives to sexually active teen-agers. Should the schools do this? Should the state or federal governments do it? Are parents to be informed of the practice? The question which people ask is this: are we combatting teen-age pregnancy or encouraging teen-age promiscuity?

As in all questions which touch our sexual lives, emotional factors here are very strong, and it often seems that decisions are made on the basis of how people feel they will be perceived, rather than on the basis of a realistic assessment of the values which can be protected and promoted. Once again, at least for Catholics, the problem is partly that of mortal sin (the category in which all forms of premarital sex were placed); can we even seem to be encouraging mortal sin?

But, as we have seen, "sin" (as this term was usually understood—the violation of law) is neither a theologically sound nor practically effective way of dealing with problems of sexual conduct. It is far better, in sexual questions, to present sexual love (with its elements of permanence and exclusivity which imply marriage) as the ideal, and then to tell people (among them, teen-agers) what to do, if they fall short of that ideal, *in order to prevent greater harm.*

There is another great advantage in seeing marital, sexual love as an ideal; we would then be able to state clearly that abortion represents an incomparably greater destruction of value, than does contraception, and we would be able to confront the abortion question *realistically.* If Catholics are perceived as being 100 percent against abortion and 100 percent against contraception, the rest of the world may be pardoned for wondering what universe we are living in. If we are to remain 100 percent against abortion (and I believe that we should), then we cannot continue to reject the one approach which will make abortion unnecessary—namely, effective methods of contraception. We have been pushed into an unfortunate position which is not even consistent with the principle of choosing the lesser of two evils.

It is undoubtedly easier to state an ideal realistically if we believe in it, and it is probably the case that sexual love, as we defined it in chapter four and since, has not been seen as an ideal by Christians, because of the anti-sexual bias of the Greek philosophy which for so long was the filter through which biblical teaching on sex had to pass. But if we do see it as an ideal, we will be able to state it, calmly but powerfully, to our children and our students, because we believe it and try to live it. If we see it as an ideal, we will have confidence in its power to motivate others, without histrionics and without our feeling the need to make those who reject it feel guilty. If we see it as an ideal, we will calmly face the fact that many people will not see this, either through their own fault or for other reasons; and then we will be able to give them some good practical advice about what to do, in order to prevent even greater harm.

In this connection, when we reflect as members of the church on the problems connected with birth control, women should be heard (as they have not been in the formulation of papal teaching up to the present). Women have a sense of the creativity of human sexuality and of the essential union between the biological and the spiritual components of human sexuality. Their judgment on the appropriateness of various means of birth control should be listened to by all in the church; and within each marriage, the husband should strive to be as sensitive as possible to his wife's feelings in these matters and as alert as possible to her insights.

The Question of Papal Authority

The question of birth control in the Catholic church today is probably much less a question of sexual morality than it is a question of church authority, and of the sources, limits, and binding character of that authority. Pius XI and Pius XII never formally claimed infallibility for their teaching against contraceptive practices, and neither have their successors, but their teaching was usually characterized as an exercise of the "authentic, ordinary magisterium" of the church—that is, the exercise of the divinely authorized teaching power, to which all Catholics owed obedience. What this meant in practice was that their teaching was regarded by most Catholic theologians as irreformable and therefore as practically infallible. It is very difficult for these theologians, and for all who were trained in the seminaries where such views held sway, to envisage any change in the doctrine, without calling into question papal infallibility itself and, more generally, the authority of the church in moral matters.[90] It is this fact which underlines the tragic paradox of Paul VI's encyclical, *Humanae Vitae*; a major motive in writing the letter was probably the desire to avoid any erosion of papal authority, but it is certainly clear by now that this encyclical has caused the greatest authority crisis in Catholic Christianity since the Reformation.

Is there any possibility that what is called the "official" position of the Catholic church on birth control will change? It is clear that the laity have largely abandoned the traditional teaching. One of the most thorough and responsible studies of the question, conducted by the priest and sociologist Andrew Greeley, found that in the United States 96 percent of Catholic couples in their twenties did not think that contraception was wrong, and this view was shared by 87 percent of those in the same age group *who were weekly communicants*. Less than one-third of the priests surveyed (in all age groups) agreed that contraception was always wrong. In the period following the publication of *Humanae Vitae*, which extended the previous condemnation of artificial birth control to include the newly discovered contraceptive pill, a few national conferences of Catholic bishops cautiously and tactfully expressed their reservations about the teaching of the two Pius's and Paul VI. If Vatican authorities insist on trying to force a return to the pre-Vatican II situation, they will be attempting the impossible. The laity have rejected the traditional teaching, and those priests who are working in the parishes and are in immediate contact with the laity do not seem prepared to enforce the teaching, either in the confessional or in premarital counselling. Of course, if contraceptive intercourse were really a serious violation of God's law, the fact that large numbers of lay-people, priests, and even bishops are unaware of this fact would be quite irrelevant. However, the fact that the "official" Catholic position rests not on divine positive law, or on anything in the Old or New Testaments, but on the so-called *natural* law, which is, in principle, accessible to all, does force us to ask why so few people see the cogency of this "official position."

Is There Any Way Out of the Impasse?

Is there any way of resolving the disagreement? Finding such a resolution may be one of our most important tasks during the next twenty years, if large numbers of American Catholics are not going to simply drift away from a church which they perceive as having lost contact with the real world. If a way out of the impasse is found, this will come about, not through finding some "golden mean," a hidden key to a compromise which has eluded all for the past fifty years, but rather by taking two questions very seriously. The first question is this: what are the specific values connected with human sexuality, which the papal teaching has tried to safeguard and protect? The second question is a related one: can we distinguish real commitment to these values from the traditional philosophical and theological framework in which such commitment has been expressed? These questions are both important, and if we take them seriously, we will have to question many of our assumptions, no matter which "side" we are on. Those who objected to Paul VI's encyclical, *Humanae Vitae,* will have to make an effort to see the positive values of the letter. Those who support the papal teaching will have to try to see that some elements of the teaching may be considerably better than the framework used to support the teaching as a whole.

The Values Safeguarded by the Papal Teaching

There is no method of birth control which is not flawed in some respect. Some of them simply do not work very well and they create anxiety for that very reason. Others interfere rather crudely with the spontaneity which is proper to our sexual lives and impose on married people an almost unnatural programming of their emotional lives. Still others pose uncertain health hazards. All of them superimpose technical and rational planning on a human act which ideally should manifest and realize nothing but personal love and the total commitment of husband and wife to each other. (Note carefully that it is not the use of *intelligence* which creates the problem here, but the invasion of *technical reason* into the most intimate sphere of human life.) The total openness of this commitment is a high value, and I believe that the defense of this value was at least *one* major concern of Paul VI in *Humanae Vitae.*[91] One of the tragedies of Paul's pontificate was that the theology of marital intimacy which the letter contained, went unnoticed in the uproar over his condemnation of the recently marketed contraceptive pill.[92] This was unfortunate for a variety of reasons. Not the least of these is the fact that we *need* a view of marital intimacy as an event which should engage us totally as persons, and therefore as an event which can never fully "make its peace" with the invasion of technology, pharmaceutical or otherwise, into this most profoundly personal domain. *Humanae Vitae* does make this point, and the encyclical should be read and reread, so that we can develop an esteem for precisely that facet of its teaching. In terms of the ideals which should be realized in the marital relationship, Paul VI's words are a strong statement that non-con-traceptive intercourse constitutes precisely such an authentic ideal. The Pope obviously intended to state something *more* than this, something which would exclude contraceptive intercourse. That is beyond question and not a point of disagreement here. But his words show that, at the very least, and to put it negatively, the contraceptive mentality is inimical to the dynamisms of sexual love itself.

The Philosophical and Theological Framework in Which This Ideal Has Been Expressed

Although *Humanae Vitae* included, for the first time in a papal document,[93] a fine statement on the meaning of marital intimacy,[94] the Pope went on to deal with the contraceptive pill, using the traditional natural law terminology of the past centuries (an approach to natural law which was *not* that of Thomas Aquinas, although many who used this terminology claimed his support). The traditional terminology which the Pope used did not see human conduct in terms of responsibility for realizing an ideal, but rather in terms of obedience to law as a way of staying out of sin, and it was in regard to sexuality that this approach did the greatest harm.[95] However, it is precisely in this concentration on sin as a violation of law,[96] that moral reflection lacked a solid biblical basis, particularly in the material in the Gospels which goes back to the historical Jesus, and in the authentic Pauline epistles.

Law developed in human society as a means of regulating external conduct, and it did this for good reason: it is in our external conduct that we are most manifestly unjust to each other, and it is this injustice which law is designed to prevent. However, when law is used as a means of dealing with human sexuality, with sexual intercourse itself, and with the problem of contraceptive practice, it will inevitably emphasize the external, biological integrity of the marital act and will tend to label anything which interferes with that biological integrity as a violation of the law of God.

With the emphasis on law went a notion of sin as the violation of law, and this in turn raised the question of how serious the law was, which was being violated. In most areas of moral concern, church teaching and the moral tradition itself admitted that, although some violations of the law were, of their very nature, *grave* or serious, other violations of the law were inherently not grave, not so serious, because they did not so seriously compromise the value which the law was designed to protect. However, in the domain of sexuality the moral tradition made no exception. Only there did it assert that *all* violations of the law were, of their very nature, grave, or, in the terminology which was current, "grave objective moral evil," and that for this reason, presuming sufficient reflection and full consent of the will, the choice to act in such a way was always seriously sinful, always a mortal sin. This was expressed in the dictum, "in matters of sexual morality, there is no parvity (smallness) of matter."

Why this peculiar exception in sexual matters? There seem to be two reasons, the first of which makes a very important statement about human sexuality, and manifests a concern, in the absence of which sexuality will not be fully human. As we have pointed out again and again, sexuality is not at the periphery of human personality; sexual expression manifests the *self*, the total person, in a peculiarly intense way. Sexuality is an essential aspect of our human condition, and it engages the center of the personality in a way that other spheres of life do not. This is the strength of the traditional teaching about "no parvity of matter." The modern adage to the effect that our sexual activities have nothing to do with the kind of persons we are is profoundly untrue and represents a trivializing of sex which leads to a trivializing of the self.

On the other hand, is it really true that there are *no* forms of sexual behavior which fall short of the ideal, yet are not inherently grave or serious, either because of the circumstances in which they occur, or because they simply do not negate the real purpose of human sexuality to the same degree or in the same way as other forms of conduct do? It seems clear that rape or the sexual abuse of children both have an inherent seriousness about them which sets them worlds apart from the almost inevitable transitory stage of masturbation through which the male adolescent passes, or from the sexual relationships of older people, not married to each other, who find in them some surcease from loneliness.

This question would probably receive a simple and obvious answer, were it not for one obstacle. This brings us to the second reason for which traditional moral teaching allowed no parvity of matter: the rather strong anti-sexual bias, which the church inherited from platonic and stoic philosophy. This anti-sexual bias was expressed in Gregory the Great's assertion that the pleasure experienced in sexual intercourse was, in itself, mortally sinful, and that it was only saved from this if done in marriage and for the purpose of procreating a child.[97] Suspicion of sexual pleasure in *all* forms, even between married people, was a major factor in emphasizing the seriousness of all sexual sins. It was this, together with a natural law theory which emphasized the physical integrity of the marital act, which forced the moral tradition to assert that, while certain forms of sexual activity were, in and of themselves, more serious violations of the natural law than others, nevertheless, *all* violations of the natural law in sexual matters were inherently on the "mortal" side of the line which separates mortal from venial sin. But it is precisely this position which lacks a solid New Testament pedigree, and which is hard to maintain, if Thomas Aquinas' theory of natural law is applied to the data, as we know and understand it today.

After everything has been said about non-contraceptive intercourse as an ideal in marriage (and obviously not everything has been said), we have to admit that in human life values can be in conflict, and different ideals may not be simultaneously attainable. When the conflict is real, we are called to make a conscientious judgment which embodies our best attempts to locate the values which are greater and to choose them, while doing all in our power to minimize the harm which will come about through the inevitable neglect of the lesser values. Traditional moral theology could not do this in sexual matters, and specifically in regard to contraception, because the "no-parvity-of-matter" mentality stamped contraceptive practices not as "falling short of the ideal" but as "objectively grave evils," which can never be the object of a good moral choice. It is *this* principle ("no-parvity-of-matter") which constitutes the overriding obstacle to a reasonable solution to the problem of contraception. Moreover, this principle does not deserve our allegiance for two reasons: it lacks a good New Testament pedigree, and it reflects the sexual pessimism of stoic thought and the antipathy to sex which characterized platonism in all periods. The important value which this "no-parvity" principle strives to protect (that is, the fact that sexuality is not on the periphery of our lives but is central to our personal existence) is better protected by a moral theology which sees truly human sexual expression as an *ideal* which we hope to approach, rather than as a law, each and every violation of which must be stamped as mortally sinful.

Non-contraceptive intercourse is an ideal, the attainment of which can be limited by many factors.[98] In practical life, contraceptive intercourse, although not an ideal, could be morally chosen on the grounds that it is the option which will best foster and promote sexual love in the concrete situation. If this approach is taken, it will not represent the triumph of "morality by consensus," because ways of acting do not become worthy of being chosen, and moral choices do not become good, simply because there is a strong consensus on the issue. The significance of the strong consensus among lay Catholics on the issue of birth control is that it gives us reason to doubt the interpretation of the natural law on which it rests. Rudimentary honesty demands that we stop speaking of natural law as though it were inscribed in human nature, when only a small minority of men and women (even in that church in which this natural law theory developed) can perceive what its demands really are. If nature and the evidence which it puts at our disposal were so wanting in probative power, then it would seem that we would rightfully look to revelation, to biblical sources, to supplement its absence. But precisely this is what the papal teaching itself has never claimed

8.

Sexual Love and the

Celibate Vocation

The positive treatment of sexual love in this book naturally raises the question of the degree to which human fulfillment is possible for those who choose to enter *religious life*: that is, a life, chosen by some Catholics (and a few members of Protestant churches which recognize the practice), which includes the commitment not to marry and to renounce every form of voluntary genital sexual activity "for the sake of the kingdom"—that is, for God and for the spreading of his reign over the earth. Members of religious orders are bound, explicitly or implicitly, by three vows or promises of poverty, chastity, and obedience. It is, of course, the second vow which is of special interest to us here.[99]

In the decade after the Second World War, two Jesuit theologians, John Courtney Murray in the United States and Karl Rahner in Germany, raised some serious questions about these vows. Both pointed out that the vows, though good in themselves, could create serious problems for those who took them, unless these people had already reached a certain level of emotional maturity. They argued that there were serious dangers connected with the vows and that these dangers consisted in the fact that each of the vows exempted a man or a woman from one of the creative tasks and challenges essential to achieving psychological maturity. They pointed out that part of our human task is to learn how to use and enjoy material things without being dominated by them, and that the vow of poverty can simply exempt the religious from learning how to make these choices. They pointed out that part of our human task is to discover the real meaning of freedom and to learn how to exercise a properly human autonomy without becoming "laws unto ourselves," and that the vow of obedience may simply exempt the religious from this difficult and rewarding task. And they pointed out that part of our human task is to engage in the creative encounter with the opposite sex, to develop a sense of our own identity, and to become true and complete selves precisely in that encounter. And they pointed out that the vow of chastity may simply remove the possibility of this creative and challenging encounter, leaving the religious with a partial or fragmented identity. (This would be a great danger, especially if the man or woman entering religious life had been deprived of normal contacts with the opposite sex during adolescence.) In recent years, the discussion has centered more and more on the problems posed by celibacy and by the vow of chastity, and this is probably a good thing. Each of us exists as man or woman in all dimensions of our lives. We are persons either as men or as women, and the achievement of human personality has much to do with achieving a creative dialogue with the opposite sex.

An older moral theology had been able to justify sexual expression only for procreation and had left all other facets of human sexuality under the shadow of sin. In such a world, avoidance of sexual activity was a positive good. On the other hand, more modern tendencies in moral theology suggest that sexual love is a good in itself and agree that the genital expression of sexual love should foster and promote this love and lead to true psycho-sexual maturity. Inevitably, this new emphasis on marriage and sexual intercourse as a true good for husband and wife raised the question of whether those who do not marry might be abandoning something essential for psycho-sexual maturity. These questions, in turn, have prompted a considerable amount of speculation about the meaning of sexuality for the celibate. Some of this speculation has been profitable and has led to positive results. Some of it has been silly and even harmful.

The question of the possibility of true maturity for those who choose not to marry in order to pursue a religious vocation is one that merits very serious thought and discussion. This is especially true in view of much of the pop-psychology which is aimed at religious today in the form of articles, workshops, and the like. Much of this stems from the fads of the sixties and the early seventies and from the psycho-babble which "articulated" these fads: "Let it all hang out," "Don't be ashamed of your body," "Reach out and touch someone," etc., etc. The peculiar abhorrence of privacy which surfaces in all of this nonsense is not a sign of a healthy attitude toward one's own body or toward human sexuality. More often than not it is a sign of an identity problem and of the absence of psycho-sexual maturity.

The question of personal identity and psycho-sexual maturity for the man or woman in religious life is a serious one, even though it can easily be misunderstood. The man or woman who has ostensibly given up marriage for the sake of the kingdom and then engages in a self-centered search for "personal fulfillment" as a very private and personal possession is no less tragi-comic a figure than the husband or wife who is prepared to *use* his or her marriage partner in the ultimately selfish search for "personal identity." What we said earlier about the essential human mystery—that we find ourselves only in giving ourselves totally to another—is just as true here. The discovery of self is very much like the experience of every pleasure which is truly human: it is a by-product of a creative act, but if sought for itself it will never be found. In marriage, as in religious life, those who *seek* self-discovery are on a hopeless quest; but if they seek the other whole-heartedly and single-mindedly, they will receive, as pure gift, the only self that is worth having and being, and they will be fulfilled beyond their dreams.

In addition to the good and serious questions about the relationship of religious life to human sexuality—questions which, if answered honestly, can lead to a new understanding and esteem of religious life, there are other objections to the religious vocation which come from a distorted view of human sexuality. Religious life seems weird and incomprehensible to those who identify human fulfillment with instant gratification of every fantasy, or who see sex as a spectator sport or as an activity for gourmets or erotic engineers. Objections from this corner hardly need be taken seriously (although religious life may lose some of its attractiveness to Christians who, often unconsciously, adopt the ethos, the value system, of the media and of the contemporary world which is so much the product of this zealously propagated value system).

A Questionable Defense

In the face of these many questions about the power of religious life to promote the integration of the human personality, there has been a tendency in recent years to explain and justify the religious vocation on the basis of *activity* (preaching, teaching, nursing, missionary work)—that is, to justify it on the basis of service to the church, the people of God.

Now it is clear that the tasks in question are important, even essential, but it is reasonable to ask whether they are really different if done by religious. At least much of the time, I believe that the honest answer is that the individual lay(wo)man can be just as effective in fulfilling any of these tasks as can the religious, although it is true that a religious order can bring a corporate and institutional commitment, a continuity, to a task, which would otherwise be performed in a haphazard way, if at all. (And this seems to be particularly true of teaching.) In any case, even if there is something unique which the religious brings to these tasks (and, as we will see, there may be), this happens not precisely because the religious has chosen a "service" vocation, but because of something much deeper and more essential in the religious vocation itself. (And unless religious see this clearly, they will feel threatened by lay Catholics who are perceived to be doing one or another of the tasks to which the religious orders were traditionally devoted, and to be doing it just as well as the religious themselves. Members of religious orders who are clear about who they really are and to what they are really called, are not threatened by such a phenomenon; rather, they welcome it.)

It is also important to see that the attempt to justify the religious vocation in terms of service really sidesteps the question of the human fulfillment of the religious. If those entering religious life were to be deprived of opportunities essential for psycho-sexual maturity, it would be hard to find any justification for a life which demanded so great and so destructive a sacrifice. If religious life is not meaningful in itself and in terms of the truly human fulfillment it can bring, then nothing can justify it. For this would be to relegate the religious (wo)man to the status of a mere means and such a form of religious totalitarianism would be profoundly unchristian.

A Deeper View

This discussion implies that the deep meaning of religious life (deeper, even, than the vows, because it precedes them, supports them, and can even exist without them) lies in the special kind of relationship with God to which it is a call. Many different activities and kinds of service can flow from this relationship, but all of them are distinct from the relationship and cannot be identified with it, precisely because the relationship itself is the ground and source of all of them. This special relationship with God is closely connected with that element which seems to characterize (especially to public view) the life of the religious: the decision to remain unmarried for the sake of the kingdom, for the sake of God. Note carefully that this is not to say that *not* marrying, *not* engaging in sexual activity, is the heart of a religious vocation; this would be a very negative approach, (but it is one which has given to the words "celibacy" and "religious chastity" their negative connotations). But the decision to remain unmarried has much to do with what is essential to a religious vocation, precisely because of the *positive* basis of such a decision. Paradoxically, we can come to understand this positive element better by turning to that very development which seems to pose such a threat to the validity of religious life in our day—that is, to the high value placed on sexual love in contemporary Christian thought, and to the increasingly positive evaluation of sexual expression as a way of fostering love and thereby perfecting husband and wife. (This development poses such a threat, of course, precisely to the degree to which religious have seen their vocation as service-oriented and have seen the married vocation as "person-oriented." Unless this essentially false dichotomy is overcome, religious life has no future.)

There is a question, therefore, of whether it is possible to reconcile the high value of sexual love and its great importance for personal fulfillment, with that choice which Christian faith has inspired some men and women to make from the very earliest times: the choice to remain unmarried for the sake of the kingdom. The same question can be asked in another form: since we become persons as men or as women, and since sexual love seems to play an essential role in this process, what happens to those who deliberately choose not to achieve sexual love in their lives? Is there any substitute for it, anything which can replace it?

Note here that what is under discussion is not the celibacy of the secular, diocesan priesthood. The free choice to forego marriage for the sake of the kingdom should not be confused with a law which obliges those who wish to serve the church as priests to renounce marriage. It would, of course, be perfectly possible for one who had chosen to remain unmarried for the sake of the kingdom to *also* be called to the priesthood and to respond to that call, but priesthood as such has no necessary connection with the unmarried state. On the other hand, religious life, in the sense in which the term is used here, does involve the decision to remain unmarried for the sake of the kingdom. And when this decision is properly understood and motivated, it is very central to religious life.

The Heart of the Religious Vocation

The key to understanding religious life is the insight that sexual love is a very high value, but in the strict sense of the word, it is not an absolute value. It is *one* of the two fundamental ways that human beings have of being related to another, of transcending themselves in this relationship, and therefore of finding themselves in the very act of putting their existence unrestrictedly on the line for the other. There are two different ways in which God can be present to us and in which he challenges us to achieve the fullness of human personhood, precisely in the act of putting our existence on the line completely for another. For the human being called to sexual love, I believe that the word which God addresses to us could be put this way: "I give you the world and all that is in it so that you may find me and love me. I give you this (wo)man to love with your whole being, body and spirit. Love her(him) for her(him)self in peace and in joy, because in loving each other you will find me and love me. In your love, I will be revealed to each of you and through you to the whole world." Sexual love in this sense is certainly the experience of God as the source and ground of all that is, and especially as the source and ground of this other person, whose (wo)manly being is perfectly complementary to my own.

However, this is not the only possibility. God can be present to us not only as the one who is revealed in this other human being whom he gives us to love, but in another way as well, and it is this other way which is the key to the religious calling. God can be for a man or a woman that *one "other,"* who fulfills them precisely as persons. God is a person—one who knows and is known, loves and is loved, speaks a word and can hearken to the word of another. Such a God is not only father; s/he is the ground and source of all that is good in all human relationships: mother, father, sister, brother, lover, friend. (The biblical image of God as father, if taken in an exclusive sense, is a relic of a patriarchical social system and is therefore historically and socially conditioned.)

God is the ground and source of all that is real in human personality, in both its manly and womanly forms. God is the living source of what is creative, distinctive, and unique, in woman as well as in man. God is the ground of the eternal feminine and the eternal masculine. God transcends sexuality, but only in the sense that s/he is not limited to any of the particular forms which sexuality takes in the created world. God's own being embraces that total polarity of which sexual love is the created reflection and revelation. God can approach man and woman precisely as the perfect expression of that fully complementary "otherness" which, as human beings, we need in order to become persons. When God does, we are claimed in a way which is analogous to the claim of sexual love.

And it *is* God who approaches us. It is God who takes the initiative, as Paul never tires of telling us on almost every page of his letter to the Romans. He loved us while we were sinners. He claimed us, although we had done nothing to ground that claim. He is *for* us so totally that there is really no one (who counts for anything) against us. Our very identity consists in the fact that we are claimed by him and belong to him. For Paul, to be a person is to recognize that claim, to let God be the one he wants to be for us, to let him be the one who accepts, affirms, sustains, and supports us without bound or limit. This is what Paul means by faith, and it is the only foundation on which a truly human life can be built. For the religious man or woman it has a unique shading, because religious life, if it is anything, is a total response to that claim, and therefore a peculiarly total act of faith.

When God approaches the human being in this way, then that human being is involved in his/her total personality with one "who will not pass away even if heaven and earth pass away" and with one who "shakes the foundations" of the created world and relativizes all of its structures. Friedrich Wulf makes these excellent comments on this aspect of religious life:

"Religious life is first and foremost a declaration of loyalty to God, to the one and only God who is 'all in all' (1 Cor 15:28) and who is 'the one thing necessary' (Lk 10:42). God alone is the ultimate justification for religious life: God alone who is the ultimate and absolute one and who can be compared with nothing; God who is the beginning and the end, the promise and the fulfillment, who lays claim to us in all dimensions of our humanity. The religious orders today are called on to be present to the world and to see their vocations as lives of service which should liberate them for their fellow human beings and for their needs. But despite this, the ultimate theological source of religious life is indicated by the words 'God alone' in such phrases as 'serving God alone' (soli Deo servire), 'being dedicated wholly to God' (soli Deo vacare). This has been a constant element of the religious tradition from the very beginning."[100]

This special kind of relationship which Wulf alludes to has happened thousands of times in the past. It is happening now and it will happen in the future. It is a special charism and calling, and the fact that it occurs is a sign that the church is healthy and is being true to its mission (although it is important to note that quantitative criteria do not apply: the church is not healthy because religious are numerous, but because those who choose this way of life understand it and are loyal to its demands).

The special relationship with God which is the foundation of religious life is, ideally, all-absorbing and all-fulfilling. The man or woman is claimed in his/her total being by one who is the ground of all that is, and whose love brings all of the fulfillment which might ever be found in manly or womanly love. The man or woman who is claimed by God in this way turns to God with a totality which is found, in inner-worldly terms, only in sexual love. I believe that it is the perception of this which accounts for the remarkably frank sexual imagery which we find in the Old Testament, when the writers try to illuminate the mystery of God's love for Israel and Israel's love for God. The mystery of human sexuality is rooted in God, and the person for whom this God is the all-absorbing "other" can live, in faith, a mystery of which human sexuality in the domains of libido and eros are a real but pale reflection. If God turns to anyone in this way, then that person feels the need to respond by giving his/her total self. This is what Ignatius Loyola talked about in his little book of *Spiritual Exercises*, especially in the meditation on the "Two Standards": God's "needs and desires and cares," or simply "God's will," become my own needs, desires, cares, will. This absolute priority of God does not set the religious against the world; it simply means that from now on, the whole world belongs to God and is populated by his suffering and needy people.

The man or woman who is loved in this way is challenged and claimed *as* man or woman, in his masculinity, in her femininity, even though the specifically physical dimensions of human sexual love are absent. But they are absent not because they are negated, but because in these cases, the man or woman is claimed by a love which *transcends all creation* and which, in virtue of that very fact, *demands a sign of that transcendence*, precisely on the level of love. This is what is often referred to as the eschatological meaning of the choice to remain unmarried for the sake of the kingdom. Ideally, the religious celibate is willing to live out the mystery of love in faith and in hope, but in this proleptic, anticipatory form, the love of the religious man or woman contains within itself the fullness of created love in its manly or womanly forms. It is precisely this aspect of "being in love with God" which made it possible for the *Song of Songs,* originally a secular hymn, celebrating the joys of marital love, to gain entry into the Old Testament. (The point, of course, is that true marital love is not really "secular" at all, but is the symbol and revelation of God's love. The point is also that when God's love claims the individual man or woman totally, that person is called to a relationship with God which has a totality that can only be compared to marital love.) This aspect of the religious calling is particularly clear in the lives of men and women like Catherine of Siena[101] and the Cistercian abbot, Aelred of Rievaulx.[102] It is also evident in Bernini's sculpture of Theresa of Avila in the Vatican collection.

I believe that it is this which accounts for the authentic manliness or womanliness which religious men and women have at times achieved, even when custom allowed only the rarest of contacts with the opposite sex. (That members of religious orders have often failed in this respect and have become "bachelors" or "old maids" simply points out that the incidence of failure in any worthwhile endeavor is high; marriage is a good example.) Reflection on this can bring the present day religious man or woman a good deal of justified peace, particularly in the face of the incessant harping on the need for contact with the opposite sex which seems to concern the modern apostles of liberation more than does aloneness with God. It is true that an easy and relaxed relationship with the opposite sex is a good and healthy thing, and undoubtedly some of the older attitudes prevalent in religious orders were repressive and sick. But some of the newer attitudes are pretentious and silly.

When the religious responds to the all-claiming love of God with the total gift of self, then one of the more attractive by-products of this will be a genuine freedom with the opposite sex which is neither coy, nor macho, nor sexless, but which is relaxed and loving, without being "cute." But the religious will draw the line before such a relationship develops into sexual love (that is, on the assumption that s/he wants to remain a religious), because the total claim of another, of which human sexual love is a reflection, has been made and answered on another level. Human sexual love is a thing of great power and beauty, and it is not good to trivialize it or to play with it. To carry on such a dangerous game in the name of the "new openness" or the "new freedom" is pretentious and deceptive nonsense.

The all-fulfilling love of God, to which the religious is called, has no other support. On the purely created level, there is no substitute no compensation for human sexual love. (The so-called "hundredfold"—Mk 10:29—is cruelly and tragically misunderstood if it is forced to play this role). The kind of love of God to which the religious man or woman is called is always experienced in faith, and therefore it is experienced in a certain darkness, in which trust in the lover "stands in" for the felt experience of the healing power of that love. It is this element of faith and hope which gives to all genuine religious life its contemplative element. But note that this contemplative element is often present in a very prosaic, unassuming, matter-of-fact way. It is present as a peaceful awareness of the One for whom this life is being lived, an awareness that can remain peaceful in the midst of a great deal of noise, activity, and confusion.

The love of the religious man or woman is one which, like every real love, manifests itself in many other loves: love of other members of the religious community, love of the church (that is, the people of God), love of all human beings, or quite simply, in *love of the neighbor*. The vitality of many forms of religious life has come from a special awareness of the needs of the neighbor; hospitals, schools, missions, the reform of preaching, and any number of other good works have been the result. One who loves God as the all-claiming "other" takes God's work as his/her own in a great variety of ways. It is for this reason that religious life can often look like nothing more than a pragmatic way of getting a good and necessary job done. But on a deeper level, religious life transcends pragmatism; no one is more concerned about the practical service of the "other" than is the person in love.

Religious life is obviously not a relationship with God which bypasses other human beings. One of the interesting features of the life of the "Fathers of the desert" (those Egyptian Christians who went off into the wasteland west of Thebes in the mid third century to find God in isolation from the world) is that they did not remain in isolation. They were followed by others, who imitated their example and sought their guidance; and in time the desert Fathers themselves came to see how appropriate this was. We are social animals, and even the man or woman totally claimed by God will not ordinarily be called to dispense with human community, but rather to find support in such community as s/he strives to hearken to God's call and claim. Life in community (as in any family) can sometimes be trying, but at its best it offers to each member of the religious order the opportunity of working together to a-chieve common goals and of experiencing support by one's family in the inevitable times of failure. The sense of belonging to a team of men or women who are committed to important tasks on behalf of God's people is one of the great joys of religious life, and is a very solid (if secondary) motive for joining a religious order. The support of the members of one's community, very much like that of the nuclear family at its best, is a human satisfaction which should be highly prized.

To summarize: religious life is the state of being claimed totally and *immediately* by God. (The word "immediately" here does not mean "all at once" but rather "unmediated"; there is no one and nothing between God's call and the response of this man or woman.) Like any truly personal relationship, "being in love with God" is one which grows with the years and with the discovery of what that love demands and what it offers. Religious life is not necessarily a higher or better way of living out the faith, and it is not more holy or more pleasing to God. It is an alternate form of Christian existence which God offers to some, and it is essential to the church and to the lives of all of the members of the church, that some accept this call. And it is essential that those who do, live out this sometimes painful mystery of faith, giving themselves to the One who has claimed them totally, as only the lover can who has given him/herself in a way no less total and unrestricted.

More than ever before in the history of the church, many members of religious orders today are wondering if religious life, as it has existed at least since the time of Benedict of Nursia, will survive the end of the twentieth century; and the statistics certainly give no grounds for optimism. What this chapter intends to suggest is that serious reflection on the deep nature of religious life and on the unique kind of self-transcendence to which such a life is a summons, reveals that the religious vocation, if properly understood, would be as appealing today as it was at the time of Pachomius, Benedict, Francis, Dominic, Ignatius, and John Baptist de la Salle. The activism and pragmatism which are part of the American character often serve us well, as we attempt to translate the demands of the Gospel into the realities of twentieth century life. But in this matter of religious life, they may not be serving us at all well, if they suggest that what counts is "religious busy-ness," rather than the state of "being in love with God." This is what religious life is about, and unless there are some men and women who are grasped by this self-transcending love in such a way that their lives become effective signs of the totality of God's offer and God's claim, we will all be infinitely poorer, and the Christian message will have lost much of its credibility.

9.

Sexuality in the Emotional
and Spiritual Dimensions

Sexuality touches our existence as persons. But persons are not neuter, sexless spirits placed in sexed bodies. Man and woman are two fundamentally different ways of being a person, and it is important to discover what differentiates them in all sectors of life and what makes them so complementary and necessary to each other in all areas. Men and women depend on each other to become fully personal; we depend on those of the same sex to provide us with models for imitation, while those of the other sex constitute that mysterious and indispensable "other" which confronts us, which is complementary to us, with which we must be in dialogue if we are to attain our own sexual identity. The question of what constitutes authentic manliness and womanliness is a legitimate question, even though in the past much nonsense has been uttered on the subject, and even though women have had to suffer much injustice because of the inadequate and even ridiculous answers given.

The question is emotionally charged for precisely this reason. Women have been stereotyped, and artificial limits have been imposed on them in the name of fundamental psychological and intellectual differences between the sexes. Some women and fewer men have begun to see this and this has led to the rise of what is called, somewhat vaguely, "feminism." The word covers a broad spectrum of activities and ideological positions, but common to all of them is the conviction that women's opportunities should not be limited or restricted by traditional concepts of the "proper" roles of the sexes. In this matter, Christians have often resisted change, and conservative and very traditionalist attitudes have been strongest in the Catholic church. Some of this resistance, at least in recent years, may be due to the extreme positions taken by some feminists, and to the unfortunate and unnecessary linking of feminism with the defense of abortion and with the demand that homosexuality be recognized as nothing more than an alternate life-style. But most of this resistance is due, I believe, to the fact that since the Reformation, the Catholic church has had a distinctively Latin stamp; and it is particularly in the Latin countries that traditional views about women and their "proper" place in society remain strong. (Although it is easy to confuse cause and effect here: it may be that the traditional Catholic value system itself has been largely responsible for these views.)

The question of sexual differences on the level of personality (in our emotional and intellectual lives) has received some contradictory answers, because, under the guise of asking a single question, several different questions are really being asked. The question sometimes is a way of asking if men and women have, by and large, different aptitudes, and whether they tend to like certain kinds of work and excel in them, while disliking others and not doing well in them. The question can also be a way of asking whether these differences, if they exist, are rooted in genetic factors and are therefore the expression of two fundamentally different ways of being human, or whether the differences in aptitude and even personality are brought about largely or entirely by social conditioning and acculturation. In this matter, it is very difficult to evaluate the evidence, as it always is in questions where "researchers" are at work. Much evidence which appears to be scientific can be gathered in an already conditioned environment, and it can easily lead to conclusions which reflect the deep desires and the often unconscious agendas of those doing the research.

One point should be mentioned, because it is often ignored. If a given form of social conditioning of the sexes is found over a long period of time and in many different societies, then it is worth asking why this is the case. Does it (or did it) have some adaptive value? Is it possible that it reflects a deep and real difference between the sexes, even though there may be many warped and distorted elements in the form it takes at any particular period? Or (and this is just as possible) is it simply an oppressive structure which has arisen to protect male dominance, and one which we should therefore bend all our efforts to change as quickly as possible?

There is already a vast and growing literature on these questions and the last word has obviously not been said. There are a number of disputed areas, but there are also some facts, which, while not universally admitted, seem to be accepted by most people who have written seriously about women, their abilities and propensities, and the roles which society has forced them to play. I believe that it will be useful, in the first place, to list some of these facts, and then to point out why, although there is considerable agreement on these facts, there is still so much disagreement on their interpretation. In the third place, I would like to mention some interesting research being done by neuropsychologists, concerning the psychological differences between men and women and concerning their origin. Fourth, I would like to draw some conclusions, which are far from being generally accepted, but which seem to me to make good sense and which I believe are worthy of discussion.

Nature and Nurture and Their Effect on Personality Traits: Sex Roles

Traditional thinking about the "proper" roles of the sexes has led to much outright oppression of women and to limiting their opportunities in almost every walk of life. It is difficult not to agree, for example, with the general evaluation of the evidence which is adduced by Simone de Beauvoir,[103] although, admittedly, some of the conclusions which she drew from the evidence were dictated by Sartre's understanding of Marxist theory, and have little to do with the evidence itself. Throughout history, women have often been regarded merely as reproductive machines, and even in periods in which this statement might seem too strong, it seems clear that society has been content to define women in essentially biological terms. Furthermore, traditional views about sex roles have barred women from a number of professions, or from specific positions within some professions. In general, women have been given jobs with less responsibility, less recognition, less pay. There has been a general tendency to regard women as not very good at decision making and long-range planning, and often, as not very good at using *reason* or intelligence.

The Aptitudes of Men and Women

In very general terms, there are some verifiable differences in aptitude between men and women in a number of areas. The evidence here is strong, although it is largely confined to the western world, and it is only true statistically, and not individually, as is demonstrated by many striking individual exceptions. For example, as a group, women seem to excel in verbal skills, men in mathematical skills. Men of all ages tend to be far more aggressive than women—a fact of which insurance companies take note in charging the highest premiums to unmarried males below the age of twenty-five.

However, at least some of these verifiable differences may be the result of social conditioning and acculturation. Society has learned to condition the young and to fit them to fulfill its expectations, and society does this in amazingly subtle ways. But here, even when we become aware of these conditioning patterns, I believe that the questions mentioned above will be useful: Is the kind of conditioning in question very common? Why is it found so universally that exceptions are notable and attract our attention? The universal prevalence of such conditioning certainly does not make it good or desirable, but it does suggest that we should ask about its causes. When the causes are found, it is possible that we will find that we should do everything in our power to prevent such conditioning, but it is also possible that we may discover something quite fundamental about the differences between men and women--something which is worth preserving and affirming, even though it may have been found in a very distorted form in many or most cultures.

The views of Richard Leakey, the paleoanthropologist, are interesting. He agrees that social conditioning has been a factor in the prevalence of male-dominated societies, but he also points out that social conditioning can hardly be invoked to explain the overwhelming prevalence of male-dominated, as against female-dominated societies. To put it simply, why is the proportion not somewhere near fifty/fifty, rather than ninety-eight /two?[104]

Leakey is quite aware that there were historical and cultural factors which aided male dominance in many primitive societies. When our ancestors moved from Africa into the colder climates of the north, they had a far greater need of meat than they did in central Africa, and they got this meat by hunting large animals—something the men were better at than the women. The possession of meat was a source of power and men were the ones who had this power and used it. But then just as we are tempted to conclude that the system of male dominance rests on cultural factors and on the value system of a hunting/gathering society which we left behind thousands of years ago, Leakey draws a somewhat different conclusion, and argues that, although prejudice and conditioning undoubtedly play a role in the perpetuation of male-dominated societies, these factors are difficult to deal with, precisely because *biological evolution itself* has implanted within us a tendency and a propensity toward male dominance.[105] He does not suggest that male dominance is *dictated* by our deepest biological nature, but merely that "biological propensities which linger in our genes" incline us in this direction. He points out that, if we attempt to change the structures of society, so as to enable women to participate fully, we will not be violating some profound biological imperative, which would then wreak its vengeance on us in yet unknown ways. But he makes a good point: if there are biological factors which account for the propensity toward male dominance, we will not be able to deal with them unless we acknowledge their presence.[106]

The conclusion which I draw from Leakey's material and from much other research in the field, is that the extreme environmentalists (those who

assert that male dominance is *solely* the result of society's conditioning)
are not only playing fast and free with the facts, but that they are staking
out a position which will make the true liberation of women much more
difficult. If we can discover the causes of male dominance and of the oppression of women, then we are in a position to do something about them.
If there are biological and genetic factors which have played a role, this
does not mean that we cannot change the social structures which have per-
petuated patterns of oppression. But when we undertake the task of changing them, it is good to know what we are up against.

Different Interpretations of the Evidence

When we turn to the question of manly and womanly character traits,
we find strong disagreement on the part of those who have obviously
devoted much time and thought to the question. The anthropologist, Margaret Mead, argued that many, if not all, personality traits are socially conditioned. She felt that human nature is so extremely malleable that social
conditioning can induce almost any conceivable pattern, and she felt that
the dichotomizing of sex-linked personality characteristics (that is, the
"decision" by society that men should behave in one particular way and
women in another) penalizes all members of the society and may be a con-
tributing factor in homosexuality. (She had found that homosexuality was
almost absent from two South Sea tribes which she investigated and among
whom sex roles were not dichotomized.) However, it should be pointed
out that during the past ten years there have been some attacks both on
these conclusions and on the methods of research which Margaret Mead
employed. These attacks have suggested that Mead's methods were, perhaps unconsciously, chosen to favor her extreme environmentalist position.

On this question of manly and womanly character traits, Lois Bird[107]
and Lois Clemens[108] argue persuasively that there are real personality differences which account for the differences in views, interests, and values
between men and women. Both feel that there is an essential altruism
(concern for the other) that belongs to the very nature of a woman. They

feel that women are far more concerned with life in its *totality*, with all aspects of life, and that they have a natural desire to create a stable and secure environment for those around them. Both feel that women are more deeply concerned about personal relationships and that they tend toward a more intuitive kind of knowing. Particularly in two catchily-titled but excellent books,[109] Lois Bird deplores the contemporary campaign directed toward the denial of psychological and emotional differences between men and women. She feels that the prevalence of "non-men" today is partially due to the lack of structuring of sex roles. Her conclusions are supported by the psychiatrist, Oswald Schwarz.[110]

The Reasons for This Disagreement

I believe that there are frequently "hidden agendas" which can be perceived even in the work of honest and sincere people. These unvoiced desires and unconscious motivations can work in both ways. A man may enjoy the role of male dominance which society has allotted him, and he may feel that his position of privilege is based on the acknowledgement, by all, of real psychological differences and contrasting character traits among men and women. If so, then his research is almost certain to show that such differences exist. On the other hand, a woman may experience oppression and see it as rooted in the view that there are real psychological differences between men and women. As a result, she may be unconsciously selective in her research and may amass much data which "prove" that such differences do not exist. And apart from such "gender-conditioned" research, it is clear that both men and women will be conditioned by their need to demonstrate in public that they are "conservative" or "liberal" (or, even worse, "liberated"!).

Animus and Anima: Jung's Contribution

However, there is an even more probable reason for the disagreement about psycholgical differences between men and women. When attempts are made to find some character traits which can be described as masculine and others which can be described as feminine, the issue is probably going to be confused at the start, simply because it is impossible to dichotomize character and personality traits in this way, as Carl Jung's theory of the human psyche has shown conclusively. Jung's psychoanalytic theory points out that there are "masculine" and "feminine" character traits, but that far from simply distinguishing the sexes, they are and must be found *within* each sex, within each man and woman. Furthermore, he points out that these traits must be developed and affirmed in the proper way if the man or woman is to enjoy a healthy psyche. Jung points out that the difference between men and women is not the presence or absence of this or that set of traits, but rather the question of whether these traits are found in the *conscious* or the *unconscious* life. In man, the psychological traits which are called "masculine" characterize the conscious life, preside over consciousness, while those characteristics which are called "feminine" are present in (and even give structure to) the unconscious self. In woman, the feminine characteristics are those of the conscious self and the masculine characteristics are those which preside over the unconscious. Jung used the Latin word *anima* for the feminine unconscious of the man and the Latin *animus* for the masculine unconscious of the woman. The *anima* is thus the personification of all of the feminine psychological tendencies in a man's psyche, and the *animus* is the personification of all of the masculine psychological tendencies in a woman's psyche.

Jung has described each of these "personifications" in terms which are very significant for the question we are raising here (and which are reminiscent of the terms used by many others when trying to describe the complementarity of man and woman in psychological terms). The *anima* is distinguished by a sense of the mystery of being a person, by a deep interest in persons, and by a corresponding capacity for personal love. A well-developed *anima* endows the man who possesses it with a deep sympathy for the natural world, for its harmonies, and its claims. The *anima* is the source of a sense of the value and the depth of one's own personhood, and the *anima* gives the man a sense of the greater dignity and inherent worth of the interior life, the life of the spirit, in comparison with the life of action (a life which deals primarily with "doing" and achieving, with "getting things done"). For these reasons the man who is an artist or a poet will have a well-developed *anima*. Finally, the *anima* is the source of a kind of knowledge which could be called "connatural," or "intuitive." It is this which is the source of "prophetic hunches" and of receptiveness to a kind of truth which cannot be reduced to logical codification or rational argument. All of these characteristics, which *must* belong to the healthy male psyche, are mediated to the man and they are given concrete shape and form by all of the women in his life, from childhood on. It will be above all in the loving sexual relationship (or in that unique relationship with God which we have tried to describe in chapter 8), that he will acquire an understanding and appreciation of these needs of his nature, and that they will develop in a healthy way.

On the other hand, the principal elements of the *animus* are a desire to go out and confront the world and to face all of the tasks which this confrontation implies. *Animus* includes initiative and an enterprising spirit, and it calls for and empowers courage and a sense of honesty and truthfulness in dealing with others, which is based on a sense of one's own worth. *Animus* is the source of real spiritual depth, in which insights are compared and linked in a coherent view of reality, which can be reflected on, criticized, and communicated in rational forms. These characteristics, which *must* belong to the healthy female psyche, are mediated to the woman and given concrete shape and form by all of the men in her life, from infancy forward.

We cited Neely on this question earlier, and in that same passage he goes on to point out that precisely this relationship with her father is what is so often missing in the life of the militant feminist. He gives an almost classic portrait of what Jungian psychoanalytic theory would call the "animus dominated" woman—one in whom the *animus* has taken over conscious life and resulted, not in the strong and courageous woman, but in a kind of tragic parody of male assertiveness or aggression gone awry.

Such women want nothing to do with men, and often become chronically and organically anorgasmic for men (and this may explain the tendency among some militant feminists to promote lesbian behavior). The animus-dominated woman is frequently highly intelligent and quite capable of beating men at their own game, but this masculinized intelligence alienates her more and more from her femininity, in which intelligence is integrated with feeling and is more deeply intelligent, precisely for that reason.[111]

Jung's theory (of which Neely makes a good deal of practical use) has a considerable body of clinical evidence behind it and it does seem to articulate in theoretical terms some insights which are the common property of men and women who have lived fully and loved deeply. It would be tempting to cite much more of Neely's brilliant chapter, "The Antidote of Love," but the important point has been made: it is precisely in the multifaceted sexual dialogue which goes on all during our lives that we discover ourselves and achieve our true manly and womanly being. We are in this thing together and we depend on each other totally. It is this which makes so tragic the poisonous and adversarial atmosphere which some of the more militant feminists seem bent on creating today.

The Evidence from Neuropsychology

Some very interesting research has been done in recent years by, among others, Jerre Levy, a neuropsychologist who works at the University of Chicago, and by Roger Sperry of Caltech. The research has dealt, in general, with the phenomenon of bilaterality—the fact that the two hemispheres of the brain are not completely symmetrical and seem to differ somewhat in function. In the course of her research, Jerre Levy developed a special interest in brain differences between men and women and on the role they play in the development of their personalities. She is careful to note that the results of her research are still tentative, but they could be summarized in the following points.

First, although it is true that the brain is an important factor in controlling the output of hormones which are responsible for sexual development, it is now becoming clearer that the brain itself is acted upon by these hormones and by other secretions of the endocrine glands, and therefore develops in quite different ways in men and women. The biological data are not fully understood, but it seems that in the higher animals, brain differentiation already takes place, as a result of hormonal activity, in relatively early stages of fetal development. The hormonal activity seems to produce effects in an organ or structure of the mid-brain, called the hypothalamus.

It is here that sex differentiation is most marked, and it is from here that the sex differentiation of other parts of the brain is controlled.[112]

Jerre Levy's second conclusion is that the commonly accepted belief that women excel in verbal skills is not only correct, but is genetically conditioned; that is, it is established before birth, and is not a matter of choice or conditioning. Her third conclusion is that brain organization itself is quite different in men and in women. The male brain seems to be more differentiated; that is, the two sides of the brain differ in function, and there seems to be a greater degree of structure (which would be demanded by such differentiation). Lateral differentiation is much less frequent in women and there is much greater symmetry between the two sides of the brain.[113]

There is strong evidence from electroencephalography which indicates that men are more capable of tapping the resources of the left (ordinarily the dominant) side of the brain, and women are most successful in tapping the resources of the right side. This means that men and women *think* differently.[114] Neither is more intelligent than the other, but intelligence functions differently in men and women, and in women intelligence is more thoroughly integrated into the affective life. This different way of thinking manifests itself in the fact that women seem to have greater ability to make selective use of different parts of the brain which are adapted to specific tasks, and that they are liable to be very good at linking information which comes from different sources: for example, what people say verbally and what they say in body language.[115]

This is very similar to the fourth point made by Jerre Levy: that men are often superior in isolating common elements in the midst of changing data—that is, in abstraction. They tend to be good at mathematics and have a marked ability to visualize objects spatially. Men tend to be able to concentrate on one characteristic or quality and to find it in the midst of disparate data. They also seem more able to concentrate in the sense that they can keep from being distracted.

In contrast, women are more capable of dealing with things as wholes and have much less tendency to divide and dissect reality. For this reason, they can be more easily distracted by matters which are incidental to the task at hand, but which may be very important in themselves. In addition, women have better control of fine motor activity and they speak and read with greater facility. Women are far more sensitive to "body language" and to all the subtleties of facial expression. They are sensitive to color and they make distinctions in colors that are baffling to the average man. Jerre Levy thinks that the often discussed phenomenon of "woman's intuition" is rooted in these characteristics of her brain: the woman is sensitive to a whole range of information and sees things that a man does not.

Jerre Levy mentions that it has been argued (and she regards it as quite probable) that such a distinction of brain organization may have been an important element of the "survival kit" which has enabled the human species to remain on the planet for such a long time. If it has, then perhaps our task today is not to deny that these physiological and genetic differences exist, but rather to ask how we may capitalize on them to insure both the complementarity and the equality of the sexes, without which human life will be stripped of most of its attractiveness and charm. Equality does not mean the leveling of psychological differences.

Womanly and Manly Existence: A Final Statement

Human beings are neither pure spirits nor merely clever animals. Each person is a psycho-physical unity, a unity of mind and body. There are profound psychological differences between the sexes, which correspond to the basic physical differences between men and women. This is to be expected; it would be more than surprising if differences in one aspect of our natures were not paralleled by differences in the other.

The differences between men and women in aptitude for certain tasks and in the possession of certain skills are probably not due, in the main, to social conditioning, but to differences in brain organization. Some conditioning does occur, but it is probably a *result* of the widespread experiences of differences which are already there. However, I believe that these differences in aptitude and skills are not in themselves fundamental, but should be seen as symptoms of differences that are deeper and much more important. Even differences in temperament and character traits are not in themselves fundamental, and I think that it is erroneous and harmful to take any particular sets of qualities on this level and to identify them as normatively masculine or feminine. It is probably true that virtually all traits of character have manly and womanly variants, and that those variations which we find in the way they are possessed by men and women are derived from that deeper level which is peculiar and unique to manly and womanly existence as such.

In other words, such qualities and abilities as intelligence, sensitivity to personal values, courage, intuition, and responsibility, should be found in both men and women, but they will be present in the two sexes in different ways, in different "styles." These differences reflect the fact that the sexes represent two fundamentally different ways of being related to the world and of understanding ourselves. These two different ways are constituted by the fact that in men and women, different character traits, different symbols, and different values are dominant in the conscious and unconscious selves respectively. That is, the same character traits are present in men and in women, but they are divided differently between the conscious and the unconscious. I believe that Jung's psychoanalytic theory goes to the heart of the matter here. On the basis of his theory it is possible to make some statements about the fundamentally different ways in which men and women possess their personal existence—statements which are quite general in nature, but which are at the same time important. Finally, I believe that the physical structures of human sexuality and of sexual intercourse, are the sign, the symbol, and the expression of these fundamental differences in the nature of manly and womanly existence.

Womanly Existence

A woman's way of possessing existence and of giving it both reflect the fact that the sexual relation is fulfilled within her own body—directly and immediately in the act of intercourse; indirectly and mediately through procreation, the presence of new life within her body. There are several important consequences of this fact.

A woman is affected by sexual intercourse as a total person, in her very substance. Sex will ordinarily have for her a personal meaning; "having sex" with someone she does not care for will be an affront to her whole self, a violation of her personal being. When a woman engages in sexual activity without any element of personal commitment, this will often be a sign of very serious psychological problems and deep doubts about her own identity and worth.

In *this* sense a woman is identified with her sexuality. Although the male libido is often more imperious and demanding of immediate satisfaction, a woman is more fully and totally sexual, because sex for her designates not what she does but what she *is*. Sex is not a function which she can separate from the rest of her life (at least she cannot do this safely). To point this out is not to define woman in terms of biology, but it is rather to assert that in her the biological dimension of life is inherently and naturally *personalized* in a way in which it is not in the male of the species. A confused awareness of the fact that, in a woman, sex is a more deeply personal domain, and one which engages the whole person, is probably behind the "double standard" of morality. There was and is some injustice in the application of this standard, and there are elements in it which reflect the oppressive structures of patriarchal society; but at its deepest level it is rooted in the insight that a woman is more fully engaged and involved in her sexual existence than is a man.[116]

What this means is that a woman has a natural awareness of the creativity of sexuality on all levels. She is more liable to think of sex as having a natural relationship to procreation, but even where there is no question of procreation she will naturally see physical sex as constituting a concrete unity with love and affection, and therefore she will be aware of the transforming power of the sexual relationship on all of life. A woman lives in closer harmony with nature than does her husband, and she can and should mediate to him a new relationship to the world and to life in its entirety. A woman is more aware of life on every level, more concerned about promoting it, more conscious of the mysterious power of sexual love to promote life.[117]

As a consequence of her awareness of life, a woman has a distinctive relationship to the future. She knows that it belongs to her. The future is not something which she has to conquer or on which she has to "make her mark" or affix her stamp. For her, the future is not a problem "out there" which she can face and dispose of. The future is part of her and belongs to her, and for this reason it can instill in her a sense of deep foreboding and anxiety, precisely because, when there is question of the future, she knows that she herself is at stake.

Manly Existence

A man's way of possessing existence and of giving it reflects the fact that for him, the sexual relationship is fulfilled when he finds the center of his being in another person. This is true directly and immediately in the act of intercourse itself, but it is true indirectly and mediately in the fact that this other person is the one who will bear the child which is also his. This fact has important consequences.

A man is not in peaceful "possession" of his sexuality to the same degree as a woman. Sex is something that he does rather than something that he is; it is more of an act than a state, and it does not touch his whole personality as it does in a woman. His libido is powerful, but it is more centrifugal and peripheral. A symptom of this is the fact that sexual activity is less integrated with affection and love, and hence he can separate them more readily than can his wife. Although his sex drive is very imperious, it engages him less as a person. (The point here is that this is his "natural" state, not that it is an ideal.)

Physical sexuality itself symbolizes and realizes the truth that man must leave himself to find himself. The male of the species is, in all respects, more outgoing and more task-oriented. In all areas of life, he is the discoverer who is called to seek and to find, and there will always be a certain restlessness about his search. Typically, for him the future is a task, to be analyzed, met, and mastered. It is something "other," quite distinct from himself, and he experiences it as a challenge. If the challenge is of just the right degree of difficulty, he will exult in it, and if it is too great, he will fear it. But he will never feel the same deep-rooted anxiety about the future that his wife does, because he can always keep that future at arm's length.

For the man, the integration of physical sexuality into his personal existence is a task. The fulfillment of this task will demand great unselfishness, true asceticism, not a little humility. If he accepts the challenge and has found the right woman (but these are really the same, because without her he will not even be aware of the task), then a great depth of personal existence will be opened up to him.[118]

Man and Woman: A Common Destiny

We achieve authentic manhood, authentic womanhood in the generous and joyous acceptance of our sexuality. We are each called to accept the kind of person that we are—man or woman—and to rejoice in all of the special capacities and challenges which that kind of personhood implies. First of all, we are called to accept our dependence on the other sex if we are ever to discover ourselves and to find our own identity. Second, we are called to accept responsibility for the other sex and for the task of helping those of the other sex achieve a healthy sexual identity and true sexual maturity. Third, we are called to understand that securing full and universal equality for the other sex is an essential part of this responsibility. (In almost all societies, women have been and are the victims here.) Fourth, we are called to affirm the total complementarity of the sexes in all domains of personal existence and private and public life (which will, of course, be impossible without total equality), and we are called to resist any tendency to limit the complementarity of the sexes to the physical realm.

Finally, we are called to accept all of these tasks in the conviction that to be a human being is to be one who is made in the image and likeness of God, and in the further conviction that it is precisely in the mutual complementarity and fulfillment of man and woman that we realize and make present in the world the One who is the source and ground of all that is good and true, attractive and intriguing, in authentic manly and womanly existence.

Endnotes

Chapter One:

1. In addition to the various commentaries on Genesis, see E. Schillebeeckx, *Marriage: Secular Reality And Saving Mystery I*, (New York: Sheed & Ward, 1965), p.39.

2. For a good introduction to Christian attitudes toward sexuality during the patristic period, see William Birmingham, ed., *What Modern Catholics Think About Birth Control: A New Symposium* (New York, 1964), pp. 35-45, "The History of Catholic Thinking on Contraception," by Dan Sullivan. This book includes several excellent articles which are far broader in scope than the title of the book might indicate. See also the very balanced treatment by Michael C. Lawler, in his book, *Secular Marriage And Christian Sacrament* (Twenty-Third Publications, 1985), pp.23-34.

3. This point is well made by two conservative Jesuit moral theologians of the last generation, John Ford and Gerald Kelly, in *Contemporary Moral Theology II* (Westminster MD: Newman Press, 1958), p.592.

4. Gregory the Great, *Epistolarum Liber IX*, Epistola 64, Patrologia Latina, vol.77, p.1196.

5. For a good summary of this problem, see Leonhard M. Weber, *On Marriage, Sex, And Virginity* (New York, 1964), p.61.

6. *Summa Theologiae, I*, 98, 2, ad 3.

7. *Summa Theologiae II-II*, 54, 8.

8. See Weber, *op.cit.*, p.64. This book, which is an excellent, scripturally based reflection on Christian marriage, is particularly good in speaking of the human and Christian value of intimacy.

9. Birmingham, *op.cit*, p.45.

10. Marc Oraison, *Man And Wife*, (New York: Macmillan, 1962), p.78.

11. Leon Suenens, *Love And Control* (Westminster, MD: Newman Press, 1961), pp.46f.

12. *Ibid.*, p.22.

13. *Ibid.*, p.80.

14. Ida Frederika Görres, *Laiengedanken Zum Zölibat* (Munich, 1961), p.28.

15. *Ibid.,* p.25.

Chapter Two:

16. Robert Grimm, *Love And Sexuality* (New York, 1964), p.32.

17. See the references, in chapter nine below, to Richard Leakey's *Origins.*

18. *Summa Theologiae I*, 91, 1, ad 2

19. *Ibid.* Thomas Aquinas got this from Augustine, *De Genesi Ad Litteram*, vii, 3, and ix, 5.

20. "Domestic society being confirmed, therefore, by this bond of love, there should flourish in it that 'order of love', as St. Augustine calls it. This order includes both the primacy of the husband in regard to the wife and the children, and the ready subjection of the wife and her willing obedience, which the Apostle commands.....For if man is the head, woman is the heart, and if he occupies the chief place in ruling, so she ought to claim for herself the chief place in love." (*Christian Marriage,* New York: Barry Vail Corporation, 1931, p.13.)

21. *Summa Theologiae I*, 84, 7.

22. Karl Barth, *Church Dogmatics III* (Edinburgh, 1961), p.149. The entire section from p.116 to p.140 is worth reading.

Chapter Three:

23. See Michael Novak's essay, "Toward a Positive Sexual Morality," in Birmingham, *op.cit.,* pp.109-128.

24. Novak, *Ibid.,* p.124.

25. Ignace Lepp, *Psychology Of Loving* (New York: New American Library, 1963), p. 5, puts it very simply: "Only a man who is capable of loving a woman and only a woman who is capable of loving a man, will be able to love God and others in a fully human way."

26. Abraham Maslow, *Motivation And Personality* (New York: Harper, 1954), p.187.

27. Oswald Schwarz, *The Psychology Of Sex* (Penguin, 1962), p.21.

28. Maslow, *op.cit.,* pp.187f.

29. Tillich, *Systematic Theology, III* (Chicago: University of Chicago Press, 1951), p.56.

30. See Ignace Lepp, *op.cit.*, p.18, for some interesting comments.

31. Maslow, *op.cit.*, p.188f.

Chapter Four:

32. The author has been talking about Christ's love for the church and he adds: "... this is the way husbands ought to love their wives as their very selves. For whoever loves his wife really loves himself. No one hates his own body, but rather nourishes it and takes care of it, as Christ does the church, of which we are members. 'And because of this a man will leave father and mother and will cleave to his wife and the two will become one flesh.' This is a great mystery, and one to be applied to Christ and the church."

33. This is also the usage in the most strongly hebraized sections of the New Testament: the infancy narratives of Matthew and Luke.

34. Paul Tillich, *op.cit.*, p.56.

35. Maslow, *op.cit.*, p.194.

36. Erich Fromm, *Man For Himself* (New York: Rinehart, 1947), p.130.

37. Moritz Schlick, *Problems Of Ethics,* (New York: Dover, 1962).

38. Maslow, *op.cit.*, p.193.

39. Maslow, *op.cit.*, p.194.

40. Maslow, *op.cit.*, p.200.

41. Oswald Schwarz, *op.cit.*, pp.100f.

42. *Ibid.*, p.20.

43. Fromm, *op.cit.*

44. Maslow, *op.cit.*, p.199.

45. *Ibid.*

Chapter Five:

46. Paul Tillich, *op.cit.*, p.56.

47. Note that learning the fundamentals of sexual behavior, including different styles of sexual foreplay, is a good and necessary thing, and it is not what we are speaking of here. In *this* sense of the word, learning sexual technique is a very desirable thing, and literature which is, in the best sense of the word, erotic, can be a great help here. It is not attention to detail

and the desire to explore all of the ways in which we may express love through our bodies which is problematic; it is rather the concentration on *our own pleasure*, as the goal and object of all our activity, which is a sign of unintegrated sexuality and *therefore of the absence of truly human sensuality.*

48. See Gerhard von Rad, *The Book Of Genesis* (Philadelphia: Westminster Press, 1972), commentary on Gen. 19: 4-11. For a brief but excellent statement on evaluating the Sodom and Gomorrah story, see Ruth Tiffany Barnhouse, *Homosexuality: A Symbolic Confusion,* (New York: Seabury, 1977), Appendix B: "On the Interpretation of Biblical Texts Referring to Homosexuality," pp.179ff. This book, the work of a psychiatrist and theologian, is superb. D.S. Bailey, in his *Homosexuality And The Christian Tradition* (London, 1955), had attempted to argue that the story of Sodom and Gomorrah dealt with the violation of the laws of hospitality and not with homosexuality, but this interpretation has not been accepted by Old Testament exegetes.

49. Paul speaks of homosexual activity as "contrary to nature, unnatural." For the Jew of Paul's day, homosexual practice was a repulsive vice, characteristic, par excellence, of the pagan. Jewish literature of the period, as well as the Old Testament itself, contain many strong condemnations of homosexual practices, and Paul undoubtedly shared these views. His harsh language reflects his conviction that when human beings reject God, their lives become twisted and lose that meaning which is reflected in a distinctively natural and human order of things. The relation of man and woman is symbolic of this ordered relationship, and therefore it is symbolic of the relation of God to human beings. Recall, in connection with this, the prophets' depiction of the relationship of Jahweh with his people as a marital relationship. Think, too, of the Epistle to the Ephesians, which sees Christ's relationship to the church as analogous to marriage. Paul's thought on this question is very important for forming a Christian moral judgment on homosexual orientation and activity, although he should not be misinterpreted in a fundamentalistic way. The attempt of homosexual apologists and activists in our day to write off Paul's words as "mere repetition of Jewish polemic," or as irrelevant to the formation of a Christian moral judgment, is not exegesis: it is wishful thinking and should be firmly rejected by anyone who takes the NT seriously. Paul certainly does not raise the question of one's responsibility for homosexual orientation, but his thinking leads to the uncompromising rejection of the moral acceptability of freely chosen homosexual conduct.

50. But the caution voiced by Ratzinger, in his letter to the bishops (see the following paragraph), is very necessary. He notes that it is important not to use generalizations in judging individual cases, but then he adds, "What is at all costs to be avoided is the unfounded and demeaning assumption that the sexual behavior of homosexual persons is always and totally compulsive and therefore inculpable."

51. This is essentially the same as the position taken in the 1973 publication of the National Conference of Catholic Bishops, entitled *Principles To Guide Confessors In Questions Of Homosexuality,* and also taken in the *1975 Vatican Declaration On Sexual Ethics.*

52. See the Press Release of the American Psychiatric Association, December 15, 1973. For a brief account of the factors which led to the APSA decision to change its nomenclature, see Barnhouse, *op.cit.*, p.45.

53. For a summary of psychiatric opinion and a detailed evaluation of all the statistical evidence, see Arno Karlen, *Sexuality And Homosexuality* (New York, 1971). This book is indispensable for serious work on the subject.

54. McNeill's conclusions have, in general, not been supported by either psychiatrists or by theologians. For a very good critique, see Barnhouse, *op.cit.*, pp.155-175. See also the reviews by J. Mahoney in *The Month,* 10: pp.166ff, and John F. Harvey, O.S.F.S., in *Theological Studies,* 38 (1977), pp.181ff.

55. For an interpretation of such seemingly homosexual conduct, see Barnhouse, *op.cit.*, p.59.

56. Homosexuals tend to identify all close friendships between men as homosexual. As Barnhouse remarks, *op.cit.*, p.26, ".. this merely continues, in modern dress, the Classical Greek habit of eroticizing friendship. This attitude does both true eroticism and true friendship a considerable disservice."

57. Barnhouse, *op.cit.*, p.28, gives the figure as "between three and five percent of the male population..." Obviously the figure will vary, depending on precisely what definition of "homosexuality" is used. For a full treatment, see Karlen, *op.cit.*

58. In regard to the supposed prevalence (and therefore acceptability) of homosexuality in other cultures, Arno Karlen, *op.cit.*, p.483, surveyed the work of anthropologists, historians, psychiatrists, and sexologists, in both East and West, and came to the following conclusions: "But we do know that predominant or exclusive homosexuality is seen negatively everywhere, and that when a society alleged to approve homosexuality is carefully studied, it turns out that homosexual acts are accepted only in special situations or times of life, and to the extent that they do not impair heterosexual functioning or imply loss of sexual identity. Rejection of one's sex role can be provided with an institutionalized role, as among the Mojave, but that does not imply approval of a happy way of life. Whenever the final limits of heterosexuality and the biologically appropriate role are infringed, the result is sanctions that range from death through persecution to harassment and mild contempt."

59. Ignace Lepp, *op.cit.*, p.99.

60. Homosexual activists often contend that Bieber's conclusions are out of date. However, there is a great deal of experimental evidence which has accrued since 1962, and this evidence tends to confirm Bieber's conclusions. See, for example, E. Hooker, "Parental Relations and Male Homosexuality in Patient and Non-Patient Samples," *Journal Of Consulting And Clinical Psychology, 33* (1973): p.140ff; W. G. Stephan, "Parental Relationships and Early Social Experiences of Activist Male Homosexuals and Male Heterosexuals," *Journal Of*

Abnormal Psychology, 41: pp.120-127; and N. L. Thompson, D. M. Schwartz, B. R. Mc-Candless, D. A. Edwards, "Parent Child Relationships and Sexual Identity in Homosexuals and Heterosexuals," *Journal Of Consulting And Clinical psychology,* 41 (1977).

61. Saghir and Robbins, *Male And Female Homosexuality,* (Baltimore, 1973). Their conclusions receive interesting support in a recent work by Richard Green: *The "sissy-boy Syndrome" And The Development Of Homosexuality,* (Yale University Press, 1987). The book contains a number of interesting insights into the relationship between effeminacy and homosexuality, and Green comes to two conclusions which are particularly relevant to the issue under discussion here. First, some boys are born with an indifference to typical boyhood interests, and this alienates them from their male peers, and often from their fathers as well. Such boys may grow up starved for male affection. Second, less time shared by the father and his young son was an important factor in the emergence of homosexuality later on. Even though Green evidently feels that genetic, parental, and cultural factors are involved in most cases of homosexuality, he describes the parental factor in terms very similar to those used by Bieber almost twenty five years ago.

62. This is the interpretation of Clara Thompson, *Interpersonal Psychoanalysis,* (New York, 1964).

63. This is the view of Sandor Rado, *Psychoanalysis Of Behavior* (New York: Grune and Stratton, 1962).

64. Saghir and Robbins, *op.cit.,* point out that even when homosexuals live in a tolerant society, their lives are ordinarily a succession of "affairs," and they drift from one to another in a way which would seem to call their deeply personal character into question. In their clinical experience, infidelity was characteristic of the majority of homosexual males who reported prolonged homosexual relationships. By the age of forty and later, the majority of homosexual men, that is, 70%, were still having an average number of four sexual outlets per week. The overwhelming majority (94%) had more than fifteen homosexual partners, while only 21% of the heterosexual control group reported a similar number of women with whom they had sex. Homosexual affairs lasted an average of three years, with only a third going ten or more years. A lifelong homosexual relationship was found to be highly unlikely.

65. Lepp, *op.cit.,* p.99.

66. For a brief treatment of the origins of female homosexuality, see Barnhouse, *op.cit.,* pp.77-92.

67. Homosexual activity in this form may have little to do with *sex,* properly speaking. Rather, it appears to be a way of *using* sex to say to the other half of the human race, "We don't need you and we don't want you." If this is the case, then this particular form of lesbian activity might be classed as an infantile reaction, in the popular sense of the word.

68. Barnhouse, *op.cit.*, p.139, makes an important point in this connection. After raising the question of whether we should assign a moral value to the failure to take all possible steps leading to sexual maturity, she continues: "I believe that the wholesale rejection of Christianity which we see in the rising forces of secularization is due to exactly the same reason that there is a strong current attack on classic psychoanalytic theory. It consists in the rejection of the idea of real personal responsibility. ... The reason (Freudian conflict theory) is under such intense attack, is because it insists that *all conduct, even when the motivations are unconscious, is the result of choice, and that therefore people are ultimately responsible in their depths.* In fact, upon closer examination, it is clear that were this not true, psychotherapy could not possibly work."

69. Richard McCormick, "Full Sacramental Support Urged for Irreversible Homosexuals," *WNY Catholic News*, 6: February 1975, p. 17.

70. Eugene Kennedy, *The New Sexuality: Myths, Fables, And Hangups* (Garden City, NY: Doubleday, 1972), p.80.

71. Charles Curran, *Catholic Moral Theology In Dialogue*, (Notre Dame, 1972), p.217.

72. For a good survey of the history of attempts to treat homosexuality (or of failures to even make the attempt!), and an evaluation of the possibilities, see Barnhouse, *op.cit.*, pp. 93-109.

73. The demand of militant homosexual activists for laws to protect homosexual behavior may well have an effect which these activists presumably do not intend. Cardinal Ratzinger makes this point in his letter to the bishops, mentioned in above: " .. when civil legislation is introduced to protect behavior to which no one has any conceivable right, neither the church nor society at large should be surprised when other distorted notions and practices gain ground, and irrational and violent actions increase."

74. For some excellent comments on the social dimensions of this particular danger, see Barnhouse, *op.cit.*, p.60.

75. For some very perceptive comments on the question of the ordination of homosexuals, see Barnhouse, *op.cit.*, pp.177f.

Chapter Six:

76. Although the terminology ("sexual love") is unusual, the content we have given the term seems very close to the meaning assigned to "conjugal" love in recent Catholic teaching, both at Vatican II and in the encyclical *Humanae Vitae*, particularly 9 of the latter document. Citations here are from *The Papal Encyclicals*, McGrath Publishing Co., 1981.

77. For a marvelous statement of this ideal, it is hard to beat James Neely's comments in his *Gender: The Myth Of Equality* (New York: Simon and Schuster, 1981), p.92: "Despite all of their good intentions, psychiatry and its handmaidens, the numerous feeling cults, have done more to disrupt marriage in the western world than all of the external paraphernalia of the industrial age. Psychiatry emphasizes self, self-indulgence of feelings, whereas marriage depends almost exclusively on selfless and unselfish regard for the feelings of those outside ourselves whom we love." Neely may cut with too broad a swath here, because psychiatrists do come in many varieties, but his comments probably hit the mark with those doctors whose clients are "into" therapy and constantly discuss it as the newest fad.

78. For a short but very clear and solid treatment of the development which came to a conclusion in the 1917 Code of Canon Law, see Michael G. Lawler, *Secular Marriage, Christian Sacrament* (Mystic, CN), 1985, pp.44-50.

79. The Council was content to define marriage as an "intimate partnership of conjugal life and love." (§48 of the *Constitution On The Church In The Modern World.*)

80. He simply states that marriage is ordered to the well-being of the spouses and to the procreation and upbringing of the children, without attempting to determine which end has priority. (See particularly 8 of *Humanae Vitae;* this represents a sharp, and not often noticed, break with the pre-Vatican II teaching.)

81. It is precisely this aspect of *hope* which suggests that the sexual relationship in the full sense belongs within marriage. There is something sad, and perhaps even a bit tragic, about casual promiscuity, when it is touted as a way of "getting to know each other." It falls so far short of the ideal that it trivializes sex and virtually guarantees the estrangement which it claims to heal.

82. But these events are, often enough, very tragic. Neely's comments (*op.cit.*, p.45) are worthy of much reflection: "Between the ages of six and twelve, a girl learns a sense of her own worth to men from her father's image of her. At this time, above all, she needs his social companionship, a developed sense of sharing with a mature member of the opposite sex that she will emphasize and enjoy in her nature all the rest of her life. .. If the young girl is denied the esteem ... that she seeks from her father, she begins, often prematurely, to seek it elsewhere ... She will do this almost any way she can to discover her worth as a social self, which unfortunately often leads to time-honored means and to one of the greatest disasters of womanhood—to precarious, premature, promiscuous sexuality. She often invests her whole youthful, idealistic self in a man she thinks she loves, and when this fails, ... she feels irrevocably damaged in her substance."

83. Neely, *op.cit.*, puts it very well: "Our real sexual gambits are intended to lead to something more than the pent-up release of the moment. However therapeutic that may appear to be, the wisdom of the ages is that man and woman are reaching out to each other for something more .... notwithstanding all modern sexual license, we all crave someone beyond our-

selves to live for and to die for. Those who claim that they are free-swinging spirits are merely at a way station where tentativeness is god. What they really seek is farther along the way, where the risk is surely greater, but the rewards become permanent."

84. Neely, *op.cit.*, 45, on ".. precarious, premature, and promiscuous sexuality."

85. The expression "many more" is, to put it mildly, an understatement. In 1979 *forty times as many annulments were granted* as in 1969. The approximate figures: in 1969, there were 700 annulments; in 1979, there were 28,000.

Chapter Seven:

86. There is some ambiguity in the term "rhythm method." Some use it to refer, in general terms, to the practice of restricting intercourse to those days when conception is unlikely, while others use it to refer to one or another specific method of determining what those days are. For clarity we are using the term in the general sense. It will then be possible to mention different ways of practicing the rhythm method—that is, following a simple calendar schedule, taking temperature readings, noting the consistency of vaginal mucous secretions, and others.

87. Different couples may need quite different degrees of reliability. Some may be interested in a reasonably effective way of spacing pregnancies; others may find themselves in a situation in which a pregnancy would be life-threatening. It is quite possible that further development of the Billings method of practicing rhythm (that is, by determining the chemical characteristics of vaginal mucous secretions) will make it an appropriate method for those who do not find themselves in a situation in which pregnancy must be avoided at all costs.

88. See the articles, "Letter to a Confessor," by Mary Louise Birmingham and "Time to Grow in Love," by Anne Martin in Birmingham, *op.cit.* Anne Martin's article contains a very good passage on the anti-sexual bias of so much of the ostensibly Christian tradition: "Sainthood and sexuality are portrayed as though they were at odds. The ideal in spirituality centered around virginity—the virgin mother, the virgin family, virgin martyrs and widowed saints. Why should the ideal be continence? My spirituality is enhanced, not diminished, by the intimacy of love. Sexuality seems to make me less selfish than anything I have experienced. To me it seems wrong to sacrifice a fullness, a completeness, a harmony between two people, for the biological part of the marriage contract. Life is too short to dwell in long periods of confusion and to deny love to another who so deserves it."

89. See para. 11: "... each and every marriage act (*quilibet matrimonii usus*) must remain open to the transmission of life." Paul VI then cites Pius XI and Pius XII in support of this same view.

90. *Ibid.*, para. 6.

91. *Ibid.*, para. 9.

92. *Ibid.*, para. 12.

93. Some may think this unfair to Pius XI, who penned some fine lines in *Casti Connubii* on the mutual help of husband and wife, but Paul VI seems to be the first to find in *marital intimacy itself* precisely such a privileged form of mutual help.

94. *Humanae Vitae*, para. 9.

95. *Ibid.*, para. 14

96. Obviously the category of *sin* has deep biblical roots, in both the Old Testament and the New Testament. But the New Testament in particular does not see sin as the violation of laws or regulations, but rather as *sinfulness*—a deep and corrosive, quasi-personal power to which we grant control over our lives. In biblical terms, sin is preeminently the refusal to hearken to the word of address which God speaks to us, and to his personal call.

97. *Epistolarum Liber IX*, Epistola 64, *Patrologia Latina 77*, 1196.

98. This ideal should be taken seriously. And it is possible that the development of the Billings method of practicing rhythm (to cite just one example) will make it a much more attainable ideal than has been the case in the past.

Chapter Eight:

99. The following pages owe very much to comments and suggestions made by Thomas Jones, F.S.C., Charles Hilken, F.S.C., and Patrick Burns, S.J. Although I do not want to make them responsible for everything said here about the meaning of religious life, their suggestions were very valuable and much appreciated. Their comments dealt particularly with the role of community life, with the essentially relational character of the religious vocation, with that *growth* in love which is just as much a phenomenon in religious life as in the married state, and with the need to emphasize that for the religious, as for all human beings, the real self is found only in self-transcendence.

100. Friedrich Wulf, in *Mysterium Salutis,* vol 4.2 (Einsiedeln, Zürich, Köln: Benziger Verlag, 1973), p.481.

101. See Barbara Tuchman, *A Distant Mirror* (New York: Knopf, 1978).

102. See Aelred of Rievaulx, *On Spiritual Friendship* (Kalamazoo, Michigan: Cistercian Publications, 1974), and *The Mirror of Charity* (Cistercian Publications, 1983).

Chapter Nine:

103. Simone de Beauvoir, *The Second Sex* (New York: Knopf, 1952). This is a recurring theme of the book.

104. Richard Leakey, *Origins* (New York: Dutton, 1977), p. 243.

105. *Ibid.*

106. *Ibid.*

107. See the work which she coauthored with her husband: Lois and Joseph Bird, *The Freedom Of Sexual Love* (New York: Doubleday, 1967).

108. Her short book, *Woman Liberated* (Scottsdale, PA: Herald Press, 1971), is excellent.

109. *How To Make Your Husband Your Lover* (New York: Doubleday, 1973) and *How To Make Your Wife Your Mistress* (New York: Doubleday, 1972).

110. Oswald Schwarz, *op.cit.*

111. See Neely, *op.cit.*, p.45.

112. Neely supports this with a summary of the scientific evidence, *op.cit.*, p.29.

113. For a more popular exposition of her views see Jerre Levy, "Right Brain, Left Brain: Fact and Fiction," *Psychology Today*, May, 1985, pp.38-40. For a slightly more technical summary of interesting data, see Jerre Levy and J.M. Levy, "Human Lateralization from Head to Foot: Sex-Related Factors," *Science,* 200: 1291-1292, June 16, 1978.

114. Neely, *op.cit.*, p.271.

115. Neely's comments on the ability of women in this respect certainly deserve the award for "most un-chauvinistic observation of the year." He points out that this ability "may also make (women) better able to perform tasks that combine two modalities in a single activity, such as understanding behavior from viewing a facial expression. It may be true, therefore, that men's brains are superior at functioning with two cognitive endeavors that are not integrated, for example, running a drill press while whistling." *op.cit.*, p.273.

116. Neely, *op.cit.*, p.161: ".. men can stand outside themselves looking in and still be successful as men; women can stand outside themselves, but run terrible risks as women .."

117. This aspect of feminine sexuality deserves much more consideration in the abortion debate, where right-to-life groups and abortion rights groups spend so much of their time shouting slogans at each other. Neely's comments are balanced: (*op.cit.,* p.263): "In short, the psychic trauma of abortion to women is immense, whatever the mitigating circumstances. This is not to deny that clearcut indications, in cases of rape, deformity, maternal distress, contagious disease, mongolism, do lessen the medical and maternal burden considerably by rendering conscious suppression more justifiably apparent. It is merely to point out the psychic truth that woman is nature, and contains within herself, very close to her soulful self, the vehicle of carrying on this life. And any breach of that contract carries its price in the unconscious where, over the course of time, psychic complaints may fester and eventually become manifest."

118. The German novelist, Günther Grass, has described the contrasting stances of men and women toward life with great insight in *The Flounder* (New York: Harcourt, Brace, Jovanovich, 1978): "Because men cannot naturally conceive and bear, ... they ... have to run themselves ragged on the treadmill known as history to make it spit out certified male products, such as dated victories and defeats, church schisms, partitions of Poland, records, and monuments... Women have no need to worry about immortality because they embody life; men, on the other hand, can only survive outside themselves, by building a house, planting a tree, doing a deed, falling gloriously in battle."